Talk Your Way to the Top
Communication Secrets to Change Your Life

Talk
Your
Way to the
Top

Communication Secrets
to Change Your Life

KEVIN HOGAN

PELICAN PUBLISHING COMPANY
GRETNA 2006

First printing, January 2000
Polish edition, July 2000
Indian edition, August 2000
Malaysian edition, April 2001
Korean edition, August 2002
English edition in Nigeria, May 2003
Second printing, August 2003
Russian edition, October 2004
Indonesian edition, December 2004
English edition in Singapore, April 2005
Third printing, November 2006

Library of Congress Cataloging-in-Publication Data

Hogan, Kevin.
    Talk your way to the top : communication secrets to change your life/Kevin Hogan ;
foreword by Richard Brodie.
        p. cm.
    Includes bibliographical references.
    ISBN-13: 978-1-56554-426-0 (hc : alk. paper)
    1. Interpersonal communication. I. Title.

BF637.C45 H64 1999
153.6—dc21
                                                                99-044997

Manufactured in the United States of America

Published by Pelican Publishing Company, Inc.
1000 Burmaster Street, Gretna, Louisiana 70053

For Katie, Jessica, and Mark
and
Mom, we miss you.

Contents

Foreword

I HAD THE FIRST OF MY THREE REVELATIONS about communication when I was thirteen. At that time I was a volunteer at the Children's Museum in Boston, which had just opened a brand-new building with—treasure of treasures—a teletype machine. It was hooked up to the world's first computer that spoke Basic, at Dartmouth University in New Hampshire. Since this was long before the invention of the VCR, let alone the home computer and the Internet—and long before I made my pilgrimage to Seattle to write the first version of Microsoft Word—a smart, introverted kid like me didn't have many choices to entertain himself. It was watch reruns of *Star Trek* or come to the museum and try to get some time to program the computer. Naturally, I spent all my time hanging out at the museum during the hours they would let me. Then I would try to pedal my bike hard enough to get home in time for *Star Trek*.

I had a friend about the same age named Stan Kugell who, like me, went on to become a player in the microcomputer revolution. He was the only one who seriously competed with me for time on the precious teletype, trying out our programs or playing the simple games that someone else had programmed. But as good as Stan was with computers, the thing I really remember about him was his way with people.

Most kids—and most adults, really—don't speak with purpose. People ask us questions and we answer, either truthfully or perhaps to make ourselves look good. We have a need and we communicate it, either straight out or deviously. We feel something's wrong and we complain, either to someone who can do something about it or just for the sake of gossip and whining. And for most people, that's life.

But there was something special about Stan, something he understood at that young age. He had somehow learned that by choosing his words carefully, by setting up attitudes within himself and steering others toward those same attitudes, he could actually influence other people to come around to his point of view.

This was a revelation to me on the order of the Virgin Mary's appearing in a bowl of Fruit Loops. I remember standing stunned, with my mouth open, as he explained to me how he intended to get Natalie, the director of the museum volunteers, to let us use the computer for extra hours. I realized at that moment that communication with other people was a much, much more interesting thing than I had thought it was, and I resolved to do whatever it took to teach myself to be as good as or better than Stan at influencing others.

The second revelation occurred when I did my first personal-growth seminar. We did a simple exercise about writing down a list of our favorite reasons, excuses, and justifications. I started to look at how I was communicating with myself. This revelation was even more powerful than the first, because I began to see that much of my life was spent in fruitless self-talk, thinking up ideas and dreams and then shooting them down with excuses and reasons. I realized that a much more effective way of being was possible.

As before, the revelation opened a whole new line of inquiry for me. I realized that with awareness comes a lot of confusion. Now that I realized it was possible to focus and apply myself at a far deeper level than I had even thought possible, I began to wonder about who I really was and what I really wanted. Some of the surprising methods I used to discover myself and live an on-purpose life became my book *Getting Past OK*.

The third and hardest-won revelation came about eighteen months into my new career as a public speaker. I finally "got" that speaking to a group is very, very different from speaking one on one and from the self-talk that went on in my head. For the first year and a half, I was performing like an actor. I practiced my smiles, moves, and lines in the front of the room. But all at once something clicked for me, and I began to see the audience as a new sort of being, one with whom I actually had some sort of relationship. My presentation became less like a performance and more like a dance.

My interest in the dynamics of how ideas spread in large groups of people let to my discovery of the field of memetics and to my writing the first book on the subject, *Virus of the Mind*. And yet most of us just open our mouths (or keep them shut) out of habit, fear, or any number of reasons that take us farther from, not closer to, where we want to go in life. It's difficult to imagine anything more rewarding than mastering these three forms of communication, not only for the rewards they bring financially but for the peace of mind and sense of accomplishment that come with having these very powerful skills.

Mastering self-talk gave me the ability to live congruently with my vision and dreams, rather than constantly shooting myself down. Mastering one-on-one talk gave me the ability to sell myself and my ideas and to have great influence over other people. And mastering public speaking brought the privilege of spreading the ideas I consider important far and wide. At the same time I was garnering quite a lot of respect from the 97 percent of the population who would rather jump out of an airplane without a parachute than risk getting up in front of an audience.

Many books have been written on success, and many more on communication. But *Talk Your Way to the Top* is the first book that teaches us to focus all three major forms of communication toward a common goal. And what a delight to see Kevin Hogan once again demonstrate his uncanny ability to see right to the heart of what's important and then communicate it in a simple, exciting way that leaves you raring to go off and try out his ideas in your own life.

Richard Brodie
Author, *Virus of the Mind*

Acknowledgments

Special thanks to Wendi Friesen for her contributions to this book. Wendi, you are fantastic!

Thanks to Tom Sullivan, who graciously gave us time for his insights into how communication plays such an important role in success.

Much of this book was written while I sat with my mom in the hospital in the weeks preceding her death. Mom was excited about this project. Mom, you were a good mom.

Thank you to my brother Fred, who helped me during this time of grief in our life.

I really want to thank people who taught me the lessons that I needed to learn in this life. Katie, you always accept me; thank you. Thank you to Jessica and Mark, my incredible kids, for being tolerant of Dad while he pens yet another work for the world. Your time is now! REALLY!

Thanks to Milburn Calhoun at Pelican Publishing Company for making this truly important project happen.

Thanks to Lynda Moreau at Pelican for the brilliant work she does in getting my work in the public's eye.

Thanks to Nina Kooij at Pelican, who makes the work I write look fabulous to the reader. It wasn't like that when she received the original manuscript from me.

Thanks to Joseph Billingsley at Pelican for his constant effort in getting the retail people to see the light! (smile)

Thanks to Jim Calhoun for his editorial work.

I want to thank my friends Holly Sumner, Mary Lee LaBay, Will

Horton, and Elsom Eldridge for their friendship and willingness to listen and carefully comment on my thoughts and ideas about this project and many others I've worked on.

Thanks to Dwight Damon for his support and promotion of my professional work.

Thanks to Devin Hastings for being a great soul brother.

Thanks to Dad, John, Fred, Becky, and Laura for your love.

Talk Your Way to the Top
Communication Secrets to Change Your Life

CHAPTER 1

Talking Your Way to the Top

COMMUNICATION IS FAR MORE THAN WHAT YOU SAY. It's how you say "it." Communication is about listening and talking and the act of mutually disclosing inner feelings and thoughts to others. As people become better communicators, they become great in everything from love relationships to business to selling.

What is "the top" anyway? Being on top means being in charge of your own life. Being on top means being who you want to be and being with whom you want to be with. Being on top means being all that you can be. When you are on your way to the top, you become known for being a great listener. You also know how to develop great friendships and relationships with virtually anyone you wish. You will certainly begin to ascend the corporate and career ladder while building passionate and long-term interpersonal relationships outside of the office. Reaching the Top in our life experiences is attainable by anyone who understands and applies the secrets of communication.

Being on Top also involves great intrapersonal communication, which means understanding yourself and participating in effective self communication. Being on top also means you are using the gifts and talents that you have been given.

People on top are happier, and often live simpler and more fulfilling lives while earning more income. This happens because truly successful people know how to channel their energy for health, wealth, and happiness. This book is about communication, and communication is your vehicle to the top!

Communicating with the people you want to share your time with is a part of talking your way to the top. If you haven't found the people you want to share that time with yet, this book will show you how to pull the right strings to find these important people. If you have found these people, this book will show you how to really communicate with them and have incredibly intimate experiences with them. Implicit to talking is listening. We'll talk a lot about listening later in this book.

For the last decade, I have spent many thousands of hours working with chronically ill people as a hypnotherapist. I have had the privilege of learning more about the inner workings of the mind and what people *really think* than almost anyone else in the world. My experience as a hypnotherapist has ranged from working with some of the wealthiest executives in the world to the everyday woman on the street. While helping people make gains in their health, I've become privy to the inner thoughts, fears, goals, and drives of all of these people. You will find no stories of these people in this book. What you will find are the many distinctions that come directly from my experience as a confidante to people who have had terrible relationships and those who have had wonderful long-term experiences with other people. You will learn how effective communication can change all the facets of your life.

For the last two decades I have also studied, researched, and learned to understand communication as it happens in day-to-day life. Although my field of specialization is normally considered to be that of non-verbal communication (body language), I have also studied and learned a great deal about people in business, relationships, and what makes people excel in the areas they need to improve on in life.

Pelican Publishing Company released my third book, *The Psychology of Persuasion: How to Persuade Others to Your Way of Thinking,* in 1996. *The Psychology of Persuasion* is a critically important book that takes you step by step through the process of influence. *The Psychology of Persuasion* was dedicated to helping people in persuasive, one-on-one communication. Influencing human behavior is critical to being truly a success in all aspects of life.

In this book, I have a lofty goal for both of us. My goal in writing this book is to share with you how to completely change your life with the most important tool we all use to create long-term and permanent change: communication. My goal for you is to focus your energy on areas where you want to excel in your life. Whether you want to feel better about yourself, talk like a winner in business, or develop great long-term personal relationships, this book is for you. This book shows you how to take control of your life and your communication in business, in relationships, and with yourself.

If you have been in business for any length of time, you know that networking is absolutely necessary for your long-term business success.

Did you know that in America's major corporations, 75 percent of all people who were moved up the executive ladder in 1998 were being mentored on their way to the top in their company?

Do you have a personal mentor you listen to for advice in your corporation?

Successful intimate relationships include those with people who communicate well with each other. The number one reason people stay together in good relationships is that they can talk and listen to each other. Being in good intrapersonal communication with your Self is our final stage of self mastery and success! The very idea of being able to be in touch with who you are is awe-inspiring. Everyone from the great success philosopher Napoleon Hill, to multimillionaire W. Clement Stone, to business and athletic leaders has had great intrapersonal communication. In other words, they have known how to listen successfully to that inner intuitive voice. They have known exactly what it takes to reprogram their mind to get what they want.

Tony Robbins earns in excess of $100 million a year by teaching and coaching corporate America to develop great communication skills. This book will show you the secrets that took Tony to the top and will carry you there as well! Excellent self managers are in touch with themselves at all levels of experience. While we are here at the beginning, let's look at a couple of key ideas that will be using as guideposts throughout this book. Guideposts are like mile markers on a highway that let us know how far we have gone. Guideposts help us remember what is really important in life.

After Napoleon Hill had interviewed Andrew Carnegie, Thomas Edison, Henry Ford, and other great leaders of his time to determine the key principles that made these people great, he found there were seventeen keys to success. One of them was the ability to contact "infinite intelligence." Like the great psychologist Carl Jung and many scientists, the truly great leaders of this world seem to be in tune with something "higher than themselves." Indeed, they were and are. We will touch on this subject in this book.

Do You Listen when the Universe of Ideas Talks to You?

All great men and women have been listeners. Bill Clinton is resilient because he has been an outstanding empathetic listener. Regardless of your views as they relate to his values and personal decisions, most people believe that he has had the best interests of the United States of America in his heart. Why did this belief permeate so? He always listened. He wanted to hear what the everyday Joe had to say about how the country could be better. The ability to truly listen is important, and we will go to some length in discussing specifically how to listen effectively to other people, with empathy.

Listening goes beyond attentively waiting for other people to stop talking. It really means getting inside of their hearts and minds and experiencing life situations from their point of view. Taking this one step further, how can we be like the true greats? You probably already know that Paul McCartney would often awaken to the music or lyrics of some of his greatest music. What was he listening to? How was he communicating with "infinite intelligence?"

Has it ever struck you (or were you even aware) that the telephone was in the process of being invented by more than one person at the same time? Did you know that the automobile, the radio, electricity, the light bulb, television, and the airplane were all being simultaneously invented (each in its own decade) by different individuals? The ideas for these world-changing inventions all were in more than one person's mind at the same time. More than being in the mind, they were all in the process of being developed at the same time. In most cases, the ideas came independently of knowledge of other people's work in the field. It would be easy to explain this fact by the evolution of industry, except that many of these inventions weren't logical or necessary *next step* inventions. When the airplane was being tested at Kitty Hawk by the Wright Brothers, almost no one owned automobiles. In fact, it was only a few years before the first flight that the automobile was invented.

What this might all mean is that the universe is out there tickling our minds, if only we would listen. It also might mean that the universe has these ideas etched into the unified field, and if we tickle the universe we might be able to scratch off some life-changing thoughts and ideas. People who have discovered their life purpose and mission seem to be able to access ideas from a unified field of sorts. Some people "listen" to these ideas and they change the quality of life on our planet. History doesn't suggest that Edison, the Wright Brothers, Bell, Ford, and the like were profoundly religious people, but they seemed to be "in touch" with something that might be described as a pool of ideas or possibilities. I believe that you can be in touch with this source of ideas. At the end of this book, I will share with you the most likely way that you can listen to this source.

Great Communicators Are Living on Purpose. Are You?

Are you open to the possibility that you might be far more than a biological animal? Is it just possible that you may have a spiritual side, or that part of yourself that is here is having a physical experience? Is it possible that this physical experience is one that should be a proving ground for your journeys and successes? If you are here for a reason and a special purpose, what might that be? People who live their lives with positive intention and with purpose are those that truly make it to the top.

Of course, most people never find their purpose or their reason for being here. Part of your purpose for being here is, of course, to experience happiness and joy. These experiences most often happen when we are in communication with other people. Sometimes they happen when we are alone in a contented state experiencing a peaceful state of mind.

Living this life can be a tremendous chore or a great gift. You may just have the ability to live your dreams and make your life a gift to others! You have the ability to experience pleasure. How wonderful it is to hold someone's hand, to hug them, to hear their voices or see their smiles. The smell of an apple pie, the scent of the ocean on a walk on the beach are all incredible experiences that we far too often overlook and discard. Spend time with people who have an impairment in one of their senses and you quickly appreciate the senses that you have.

Being "alive" is an extraordinary opportunity for learning and experiencing. The Dalai Lama has more than once spoken of a major purpose in life as being that of seeking happiness. He's right isn't he? Viktor Frankl, who experienced the concentration camps of World War II first hand, noted the importance of finding purpose and meaning in life regardless of one's personal life situation. Frankl, the author of *Man's Search for Meaning,* endured the day-to-day life of concentration camps with a remarkable sense of courage and hope. His personal attitude played a significant role in his survival. How good would you guess Frankl's intrapersonal communication was?

> *Fundamental to purpose and day-to-day happiness is our ability to communicate with ourselves and with others, and to tap that universal pool of ideas.*

In this book, we will seek to deal with the simplest of communication themes first. As you will discover, there are three basic layers of communication that are subdivided further into secrets, techniques, and strategies, but all you need to do is remember the three: others, ourselves, and the pool of ideas that later will be referred to as the "unified field."

We begin with interpersonal communication, which includes communicating with people we like and don't like. Once having mastered the basics of communication, we will talk about how to communicate with those special people we want to be in daily contact with (our boss, our employees, our friends, our spouses and children), and those we would like to be intimate with. Then we will discuss how to talk and listen to ourselves. We will learn how to discover our own unique purpose for being here and find out just how important this is to making it to the pinnacle of a successful life.

Finally, like Paul McCartney, Henry Ford, and all the great people who changed the world, we will learn the secrets of tapping the resources of the unified field in the ultimate communication that transcends physical experience into the experience of idea and thought. This "listening" process is one of the golden keys that separates those who merely aspired and those who achieved.

This book will lead you to many great successes and through the failures that make the successes even more satisfying. You now have the handbook for communication excellence that is really very little different from having the handbook for life excellence. The first begets the second. You will learn specific communication techniques and thinking strategies to assist you on your journey to the top.

The Tough-as-Nails Communicator

The question must arise, then, about how to integrate all of this into a successful business career. The answer is simple. Your job is to make your company and yourself as successful as possible. This means that you will always utilize outcome-based thinking (We'll talk more about this later!) and be willing to walk away from any deal that isn't in your best interest. You must become known as the generator of "Win/Win or No Deal relationships." This means you often will have to swim with the sharks without being eaten alive, as Harvey McKay would say!

CHAPTER 2

Talking Yourself into Success

THIS BOOK HAS BEEN A WORK OF LOVE for the better part of a year. In that time, I have interviewed hundreds of wonderful communicators who went on to attain greatness in everything from marriage and parenting to running multimillion-dollar businesses. I've also talked with people in the fields of psychotherapy and hypnotherapy to find out the most common presenting issues to therapists all over the world. Most psychotherapists agree that if people communicated better, they would experience fewer emotional and psychological problems!

When you talk to people who have achieved financial success, you will find some of the same themes that mark the lives of people who achieve greatness. First, they tend to be great communicators with themselves. In other words, they constantly are talking and listening to themselves. They trust themselves. They believe in themselves. They rely on themselves.

Second, they tend to communicate well with other people. Successful individuals from all walks of life normally have mastered the art of interpersonal communication. People who achieve greatness seem to be able to talk people into becoming more than they believed they could be. High achievers seem to have a knack for inspiring and motivating others to greatness. Quite often, the only difference between success and failure in any aspect of life is the ability to communicate with empathy, clarity, and positive intention.

I recently asked Wendi Friesen, a psychotherapist and peak performance coach, to share a few stories with you and me.

Wendi is a friend I've known for quite some time. She is an educator and psychotherapist, and she is internationally known for her work in using hypnosis to greatly improve the passionate and romantic aspects of people's lives. Her work experience includes training market makers on the options floor of the Pacific Stock Exchange. One of the things I like about Wendi is her ability to see how the past has changed her present and how seeing her future has changed her present as well! Her knack for making communication skills easy to understand is well known. In this book, she will share some of her favorite communication stories and strategies for talking so that people listen. All people on top started somewhere else, and those are the stories that I particularly find interesting! With that in mind, here's Wendi and her story about how she overcame her initial fear of talking to people on the radio:

> It was a tense moment when I decided to call the radio station. For some time I had wanted to share just what the power of the mind channeled through hypnosis could really do for people. Hypnosis can help people create a better future. Hypnosis can help people reduce the pain they are in, help them quit smoking, get better grades, even reduce the volume of tinnitus!

How to Overcome Your Fears of Communicating

Although I was excited about my work, I still was relatively new to both psychotherapy and radio. I was not likely to be perceived as being the best at communicating my ideas. When the host of the talk show asked me if I would like to be on his show, of course I said yes! (After I hung up, I said something like "ugh.") The problem didn't really seem obvious until the day before the show when I had an overwhelming feeling that being on a radio show on a 50,000-watt station might be a bad idea. Considering that I had no idea what I would talk about, had no track record of being interviewed, no book to promote, and no clue, I was left with, shall we say, doubt. The feeling of anxiety increased throughout the day . . . you know the one. The one where you think you might be sick . . . really sick. In fact, I seriously considered pulling out. I love to talk, but I was very sure I didn't want to make a complete fool of myself in the minds of all the people within a 200-mile radius of Sacramento.

Since canceling was not an option, I decided to devise a method right then and there that would get me through the evening feeling excited about doing the show the next day. Not only did I want to be excited, I also wanted to feel confident—and why not downright brilliant—in front of the masses!

I decided to "go out into my future." I decided that I would imagine I had done over 100 radio shows, all over the country, and that this was just another one, albeit a bigger one (yawn). In fact, I realized that I am almost getting bored with doing these shows, but since this one is in my local area, it might be fun and I would work myself up to be excited. I allowed myself in this future moment to remember what things I had talked about on past shows, what topics were the most fun, the sound of the laughter in the studio, how entertaining the callers were, and how good it felt to get my message out. I recalled the way that other radio studios looked. (I had never been in a radio studio in my life!) I remembered the sound of my own voice and how I always knew just what to say, at just the right time.

I did this for the entire evening, and I even imagined as I was driving down the freeway that people in the other cars recognized me from my past media appearances. And those people in the cars were very encouraging as they looked over at me with a smile and an approving glance. How did they know! I woke up early the next morning excited and nervous. I repeated my new anti-get sick mantra from my future moment: "The moment I open my mouth to speak the first word, I will be comfortable and relaxed." That mantra included the feel of a big microphone in front of my mouth.

In my moment of glory the next morning, I spoke like a professional. I communicated in ways that I didn't know were possible (for me). I came up with creative ideas and solutions to the callers' problems, and even when I couldn't offer an answer, we laughed and had fun. My future imaging worked! I referred to a book I had recently read on how our mind affects our body, and quoted ideas from it that I didn't think I remembered. I received over 150 calls in the following days, some of them just to compliment me on how natural and professional I sounded.

The most important lesson in all of this hits home when you understand that at that point in my life, you could not have gotten me to speak to a group of five people for ten minutes, let alone to hundreds of thousands for two hours. I was just like you. I wasn't a public speaker, but I wanted the experience.

Now, imagine if I had chosen the alternative. I spend the evening before the show realizing how unprepared, unknowledgable, and nervous I am. I imagine how devastating it will be when they say thank you after the first ten minutes on the air and I grab my keys to go. I focus on the feeling of nausea in my belly and let it grow. I ask myself questions all night, like, "How am I going to pull this off?" and "What if I freeze and can't think of a thing to say?" or "I could make a fool of myself in front of 100,000-plus people." I reinforce the very thing that I don't want simply because I have no tools to do it any other way.

How many times have you sabotaged your success in communicating by letting your thoughts bounce around in all of the negative scenarios?

Have you intensified your nervousness because you convinced yourself that you have nothing to say?

Have you imagined how devastated you will feel when you draw a blank if asked a question?

Using future imaging can eliminate the insecurities, the nerves, and the negative inner dialogue that can, and will, sabotage your chances of being an outstanding communicator.

Since this experience, I've learned that I wasn't the first person to use what is called "Future Vision" or "Future Imaging." Thousands of successful people use this formula for success every day. Here are the steps that the pros use to assure success in communicating to one person or a group of one thousand.

Using Future Imaging to Communicate Like a Pro

Whether you are getting ready to do a presentation for 200 people, or go in and talk to your boss, or sit down and make amends with your wife, you will benefit from the wisdom that your inner mind will give you in this process.

1. Imagine a sort of future time line where all the events and things you are going to do will be placed. Let that time line have a spot that represents the event you are about to experience.

2. Now take yourself mentally to the time just after the event. Imagine that it has already happened. Put yourself into a state of mind where you are reminiscing about the event.

3. Notice how you FEEL, now that you have said everything elegantly and naturally and have had a responsive audience. Do you feel proud, satisfied, relieved, pleased?

4. Notice how it LOOKS in your mind, now that you did a great job and communicated exactly what you intended. Do you see a happy smile on your face and see yourself excited about how absolutely brilliant you were?

5. Notice how it SOUNDS as you talk to yourself after the event. Do you hear your inner voice saying, "Wow, that was easy" or "I had no idea I would come up with such a great solution" or "I am so pleased with myself"? What are the sounds you now create as a result of the event? Do you hear your boss saying, "I really appreciated what you said. It was right on," or your wife saying "Yes, I understand how you feel," or the sound of applause?

6. Include others in your imaginary future moment. Notice how they feel as a result of how well you speak, what they say about you, they way they look forward to hearing more. Amuse yourself as you see others responding to your inspiring words.

7. What is your overall belief about the way your event went? Do you now see yourself as a confident, interesting person? Do you realize new things about yourself and your abilities to speak fluently and convincingly? Are you comfortable in congratulating yourself for a brilliant piece of work? Are you willing to experience yourself as a magnificent communicator in this future moment?

The more you allow yourself to play this game, the easier it will be for you to speak creatively, convincingly, and from your heart when you are in these situations. To the degree that you are willing to SEE, FEEL, HEAR, and BELIEVE this future moment as real, is the degree to which you can become a truly brilliant communicator.

Remember that those who are on top were not born instant successes in life. Some had life-shaping experiences that helped them to be confident when communicating early in life. Others had to learn these techniques later in life. Still others had to overcome fears, phobias, and negative programming from their past. It doesn't matter when you learn it. It matters that you do learn it. You can dramatically speed up the process by continually experiencing your future as if it is happening now.

If you have had some difficult experiences in your past that have created mental blocks, you have a choice in how you are going to experience them. You can choose to dwell on the bad feelings that are created when you think about being in a room full of people you don't know, or you can imagine the future right after that event, and purposely notice how nice it feels to be over those past experiences. Hear yourself saying, "Wow, isn't it nice to have put the past in the past? I enjoy speaking with people I have never met. They are always so interesting."

So, are you still wondering how the radio show really went?

It was a life-changing experience. When I realized what a gift I gave myself by pushing through my doubts, fears, and desire to throw up, I emerged with something that I will have forever—a new belief about myself, a belief that I can now get up and talk about my subject and have more than enough to say. I believe that our minds have access to all of the information we have learned, the books we have read, and the conversations we've had. I believe that our minds can recall the best information at the right time. This belief is a result of continually putting myself in the future moment and experiencing the outcome as real, before actually confronting whatever the presenting challenge is. My unconscious mind believes that I am comfortable talking to anyone in any position at any time. My unconscious mind has experienced these events as real, and has adopted beliefs to support those outcomes. Now, when you go into a social situation, a meeting, a presentation, or just sit down to talk with your wife, your mind will help you to find the right thing to say at just the right moment!

Wendi's account of how she overcame her fear of failure on the radio is a great story for everyone who just don't think they can do "it!" Wendi will be back later for another story about her experiences with other educators, the great, and the not so great!

Success = Talking So People Listen, and Listening So People Talk

Success in life depends almost exclusively on your ability to communicate persuasively with yourself and others. Success can include but is not limited to your income, your status, your ability to experience life fully, your ability to live within your values and principles and experience happiness and love. Most people never think of talking to themselves as being part of a success journey, and that is often the very reason that people are unable to achieve what they want to in life. Communication is interpersonal, intrapersonal, and transpersonal. We will discuss all of the aspects of success. No secrets will be left untold!

Effective and persuasive communication is the greatest of all the keys to success.

At first glance it would seem that it would be great if we could "just talk to people and have them open up." We don't though . . . and they don't either. Instead, the process of getting through to people by talking is more reminiscent of the onion. You peel off one layer after another until you come to the core, the center. Each layer is attached to the next at one point on the onion. Each layer is separate but attached at one "end" of the sphere. People have a number of levels or layers of experience. Each layer of experience has its own unique qualities that demand a specific kind of communication to gain acceptance by the person. Then, as acceptance is offered, you can go the next layer, until you reach the center where most people only sense themselves and many have never experienced at all. This is the Self. This is you, and you're pretty protective of "you," aren't you? Almost everyone is as protective of their self, and that is one reason communication is so difficult at times!

This book will show you how to communicate with other people on all levels and layers. As you will discover, **you cannot proceed to each succeeding layer or level of communication without having established trust and intimacy on the preceding level. This single fact is the cause of the majority of all breakdowns in talking and listening to people.** As you turn each page of this book, you will learn to meet people where they are in their life. You will learn how to help people be comfortable and at ease with you. You will learn how to get people to open up with you.

Talking so people listen is about experiencing your self and others completely, on all levels. The human experience is something quite extraordinary. Each day we live this life despite the challenges, setbacks, and heartbreaks we encounter in day-to-day life. Throughout all the challenges that life has for us, we have the ability to communicate with those around us to experience happiness. We can share our thoughts, ideas, philosophies, and desires. The ability to communicate is really incredibly amazing. It is through our ability to communicate that we are able to touch the hearts and minds of those around us . . . and everywhere. It is this phenomenal set of strategies and techniques that you are about to learn that will enable you to be tough as nails one day and gentle as a lamb the next.

> *Using your communication skills effectively is what leads you to happiness, love, and fulfillment in life.*

Step back and take a look at your life for just a moment. Are you happy with what you have accomplished? Have you begun to achieve that which you set out to do? Do you show love and kindness to those around you? Have you begun to make a real difference in the world? Do you have the income and lifestyle you deserve?

Today you have an opportunity to begin to live the life you chose to live. You will begin to connect with your self and with others. You will soon discover that in order to fully experience life we must become very much in touch with our true self and with the true selves of others. Today we begin to learn how to talk to ourselves and other people. Today we realize that communication is the cornerstone of happiness and love. Each communication you participate in is another wonderful opportunity to build up the self esteem of another person.

> *Communication is the key to happiness, fulfillment, and love, both yours and that of others. Today you can begin communicating with people in the manner you have known was best all along.*

Have you ever met someone (or many people) with whom you immediately connected? Have you ever said, "He is really something. I'd like to get to know him"? Now you can. At some level, you recognized something very charismatic about that person. Sometimes he or she recognized that same something in you, but then over time, or maybe immediately, nothing happened and you went your separate ways. Connecting with people is more than just physical attraction, though to be sure that is important and very real. Connecting with people really is when one person sees another and recognizes a kindred spirit.

People at the Top Connect with Others Well

Why aspire to being at the "top?" Isn't that just a 1980s, decade-of-the-self theme? Not at all. In fact, it's the opposite! It's virtually impossible to achieve true greatness as a lover, a teacher, or a salesperson without getting along with other people. In business, the ability to get along with others is something that corporate executives pay a great deal of money for! Today, at the dawn of the new millenium, corporations spend billions of dollars a year to enhance communication skills of their employees. No one can get along with everyone, but those who can build rapport with the majority will always be more successful on average than others.

There is another level of experience to consider before developing skills for communicating with others. The idea is simple: You are probably here for a purpose. Ultimately, you are probably here to find happiness and to share experiences with others. You are here to bring joy to others. You are here for one or more very special purposes.

Later in this book you will discover just what those purposes may be and how to discover them. The most successful people in the world live "on purpose." Napoleon Hill, the great success teacher, taught that you must decide on your specific major purpose before you can truly achieve success. While this may not be true in everyone's life, it is a great rule, especially for developing a happier and more fulfilling life.

One of my favorite motivational speakers is Zig Ziglar. Zig always says, "You can get everything you want in life if you will help enough other people get what they want." You are going to learn how to talk to other people so you can help them on their life's journey of success. This book will show you how to communicate with others verbally, and even more importantly, non-verbally. This book will help you become your own magical genie.

Connecting with people is a naturally given talent that has been made weaker through negative life experiences. Starting today, that is all going to change. As you walk through and experience life each day, you will come into contact with many people. Look at each person you talk with or make eye contact with and allow them freedom to be whoever they want to be with you. Give them the security of knowing that they can be open with you. You will not judge them. Finally, allow them to be inter-connected with you and separate from you. If you do this, you will become a magnet for other people.

People are attracted to the people who make them feel secure, free, and happy.

How do we accomplish such a monumental task of helping people feel secure, free, and happy? We all are so different. Different things seem to make people feel secure, for example. We have so many different needs, desires, and interests. It's not easy knowing what will make a person feel more free and at ease. In fact, we often don't know what to say when we are in the presence of groups of strangers, so we tend to simply look at the ground and avoid eye contact as we pass by. What specifically do we need to do to generate this love, this happiness, this sense of security with other people? Even when we know people, it is remarkably difficult to talk to them about certain issues and topics that are most important to us.

How do we talk about sex with our spouse or significant other? How do we talk about religion with the relatives? How do we talk politics with our friends? How do we communicate with those we love in an honest way and STILL keep the relationship intact? It isn't easy, but it can be done. (We will deal with all of these questions shortly!)

If you are like most people, you probably wonder why we all communicate so differently from each other. You probably would like some people to open up to you more and others to listen to you. Maybe most importantly, you probably already realize that as people we are more than animals, more than thinking machines, and that there is something about us that makes us special. Finally, as important as our uniqueness is, there is also a collective quality that makes us feel as if we are related somehow to . . . everyone.

This book will help you communicate to each person you meet in a way that will recognize their specialness and their interconnectedness with you.

There are reasons that we communicate the way we do.

We are all, in part, a product of our genes.
We are all, in part, a product of our environment, including our peers and families.

continued

> *We are all, in part, a product of our unique experiences (traumas, life events, etc.)*
> *We all have defensive attitudes that both help and harm us in communication.*
> *We all want love.*
> *We all have suffered emotional pain.*
> *We don't want to get hurt anymore.*

Did you know that each word said to a person either strengthens or weakens the physical and emotional well being of that person? Your words and intentions are so powerful that you can change the state of being and the state of mind of virtually everyone you come into contact with.

We must all become conduits for nurturing ourselves and others. This trait is one driving force that makes successful people so successful. We can only do this through communication. For most people in the world, our predominant forms of communication are verbal and non-verbal communication. There are, however, other forms of communication, including reading textual documents like this book and the very powerful communication in the realm of kinesthetics . . . touching.

What you say and how you say it affects not only the experience of other people, but of yourself as well. There is very little that you can say to someone that will ever be perceived as "neutral." Almost all communication is accepted at the conscious or unconscious level as "positive" or "negative." What this means for you and me as we talk to others is really quite profound. As we create positive and negative "energy" for other people, we accept the same creation for ourselves. (Jesus said it this way: "What you sow, also shall you reap.") In other words, if the words and intentions we give to others are filled with positive energy, then the effect on ourselves is virtually identical to that which was given.

> **This does not mean that if you communicate lovingly with everyone that they will love you, however. It means that if you communicate with love and integrity with all those that you come into contact with, YOU will gain from the love and integrity of what you share.**

Many millions of people are completely unable (with their present resources and understanding) to communicate in any way other than with a tone of hostility, for example. Your loving communication with an overtly hostile person will not likely result in the desired response. In fact, so many people have lost touch with their inner self that they are a detriment to society. These people often spend much of their lives in prisons for crimes of violence against others. To be sure, these people are souls and have been cut from the same cloth as you and I. The difference is that their physical experience has led them for a multitude of reasons to be careless in their actions toward themselves and others. The shell that encases that crying soul is so stone cold that the pleading of the soul for attention and security is only understood at the conscious level as anti-social behavior. It is a sad state to be in.

Your true and inner self really needs to ultimately communicate honestly, with integrity, courage, and confidence. We all *need acceptance, and if you accept others as they are, you become a people magnet.* In fact, you and I need both freedom and security. Your friends and family are craving acceptance. They are cut from the same cloth as you and I. Like you, your friends, family, and fellow workers need your love, your kindness, and your acceptance. All of us want and need love. All of us want and need to be cared for. All of us want to be independent. All of us want to feel safe and secure.

Five hours each day I work in my office as a psychotherapist. I often utilize a powerful healing modality called hypnoanalysis. People fly from all over the world to see me. In general, my practice is limited to people who suffer from chronic fatigue syndrome, fibromyalgia, and especially tinnitus (ringing in the ears). Of course I see people for other issues, including anxiety, depression, PTSD (Post Traumatic Stress Syndrome), and eating disorders, but I focus on my specialty areas.

People fly past thousands of psychotherapists and hypnotherapists because they have heard that I not only work with people who suffer from these brutal problems but that I have experienced them and for the most part have overcome them myself. I've never had to place an advertisement for the work I do. Word of mouth just spreads the good news like wildfire through groups of people who share these problems.

One element of communication I have discovered to be critically important is to listen. Listening for me is not a passive process. By this I mean I don't wait for people to finish talking and then talk myself. In my practice I listen and write down questions and follow-up questions on my notepad to constantly elicit more and more information about the person, his suffering, his internal experience, how others react to his illness, and so on. In fact, in my first session with a client, I might talk for only fifteen minutes out of two hours of total session time. The reason is simple. People are sick in part because no one really cares to listen to them. I have found people feeling significantly better after leaving my office after a simple case analysis without my having begun therapeutic "interventions." The reason? I really listen. I'm so curious and care so much about the people I see that they know they have a supporter in me. I'm someone who not only cares, but I am an advocate for their health and welfare. I am a warrior for their future happiness and health. They know that I am really working with them to get better.

When you look around at your family and friends, consider being an advocate for their happiness, health, and welfare. How specifically can you listen better without feeling the need to add your own personal stories to theirs? How specifically can you create a "safe place" for communication with those you love? You see, we actually have to think about how to do this consciously because life hasn't always been good to us. We have had some experiences along the road that diminish our ability to communicate well. We tend to start out pretty well at birth but then things start to happen, as you will soon discover.

How Do We Get to Be Who We Are?

What happens to you in this life is quite a profound experience. Each of us comes into this world with far more in common than we ultimately will have after a physical lifetime. We certainly are not all the same at birth, but we change for better and worse as life goes on. Much of what happens to us in our lifetimes hardens the heart and weakens the spirit. As we experience the trials and tribulations of life, it often makes us more distanced from those around us. The less than desirable elements of this life experience will often change our personality for better and worse. As the personality changes, each person needs to be communicated with in different ways.

Communication that reminds someone of another person who hurt him or her will result in negative responses. Imagine if you will that a woman knew a man for many years as a friend. The friend always spoke quietly and kindly to the woman. One day the man rapes the woman. The woman may develop a negative pattern of response to men, to men who speak quietly, or even to men who are friends because of this one horrible experience. In each potential case, part of each person acts to protect the whole. People don't want to be hurt again and therefore create defense mechanisms so another violent act doesn't occur. Talking quietly and kindly to this woman will not be the solution to opening up the hardened case around the soul. It will only repel you further from her. Therefore you will have to learn how to communicate to ALL types of people with ALL kinds of experiences, good and bad. What sounds like love to one is a signal of war for another.

Get Out of a Rut to Start Your Trek to the Top

We live in a world filled with people who often numb the other people that live here. We become numb to our sense of Self and our relationship with others. We're going to get out of that rut NOW!

Do you know how to do start the trek to the top? It begins with taking a look backward and seeing how we got to where we are. You'll want to understand this element of how everyone you meet has been "programmed" and just why they respond to various communication styles in the manner they do. This is pretty deep stuff, so take your time and feel free to read these next couple of sections twice!

Everything that has happened to you from the day you were born right up until the moment you read these words has shaped your life. When people spoke unkindly to you as a child, you may have defended yourself or you may have retreated. When you did defend yourself, your points of view may have been considered worthy or you may have been invalidated or even physically abused. The responses that you received to your communication changed the way you would communicate until today when you began reading this book.

How Negative Life Experiences
Can Shape Your Communication

Imagine that a little girl was physically struck in a regular fashion after she would defend herself from the untrue accusations of older adults. Soon she began to learn that it was unsafe and unwise to defend herself, and she fell into a pattern of simply retreating when she was accused of something. After awhile it simply wasn't worth getting hurt for defending herself, so why bother? The little girl grows up and she believes the world to be unfair, she believes herself to be unworthy, and she rarely speaks up to offer her opinions. She doesn't want to open up because she knows that when she tells the truth it is going to hurt. Today the little girl finds herself in relationships that make it very difficult to express her feelings. She doesn't trust people in general and authority figures in specific. She doesn't open up to those who have taken a liking to her. Her soul finds these wonderful people attractive, but at another level she sabotages herself by ignoring the communication of others, if not the people themselves. She doesn't want to get involved because she doesn't want to get hurt.

Another little girl living next door may have grown up under similar circumstances but for some reason she would fight back. She wouldn't give up, and she would take the beatings and suffer the pain. She would tell the adults and other people who would accuse her falsely that they were wrong. She, too, suffered from the pain but she grew up a little differently. She decided the world wasn't fair, that people were mean but that she didn't care. She was going to take a stand and be a fighter in life. People who meet this woman find her to be dominating, tough-skinned, and difficult to deal with. She has a hardened shell, and she defends herself vehemently against the most irrelevant accusations. She may become involved in relationships where she is in charge and accepts no negative feedback from those around her. She is difficult to get along with, and she may be an angry young woman with "axes to grind."

Yet another little girl living near the other two grows up under similar circumstances but for a different reason doesn't talk much as a child. She sees what happens to her neighbors and decides that it makes no sense to talk at all. Talking just causes fights and arguments. Arguments lead to someone getting hurt and she doesn't want to get hurt. She decides to be a "good girl," and be quiet. When you stay quiet you don't get in trouble, you don't get hit. This little girl grows up and is often very reserved, introverted, and quiet. She likes other people to be happy and not fight. She does things that help keep the peace and just wants to be liked. She doesn't really know how to communicate in any manner because she doesn't have any experience. She hasn't shared her feelings with others and is afraid that if she did she might get hurt. So she decides it's best not to talk about feelings or anything that can get her into difficult situations.

All three of these women developed patterns of communication that stemmed in part from childhood. These patterns are difficult to change, even though they are easy to spot once you understand them. There are many other patterns that are common. Some people rebel against the way they were treated as children and are consciously aware that they will do nothing the way it was done to them. Other children grow up having suffered pain and decide that if it was good enough for them, it is good enough for their children.

> *Recognizing that people are shaped by their past is one thing. Realizing that their communication skills are linked to their past is a life-changing revelation.*

When we begin to realize that all the poor communicators around us are in fact that way because they have suffered so much in the past, our attitude changes dramatically and we become more empathetic to their difficulties. You accept them more readily as people. You and I accept their weakness in communicating as something that can be strengthened. You don't take as much personally as you might have when they say mean or unkind things to you. A problem continues: How will you get them to see past your weaknesses to your beauty as a person? How will you get them to listen when you talk?

Some people of course are just "impossible" to communicate with. Their experiences have turned them into tyrants of a kind. You will learn more about dealing with difficult people in Chapter 12, which discusses Well-Intentioned Dragons.

In just a few pages you will learn how to communicate with all kinds of people.

One style of communication simply doesn't work with all of the different people in the world. In fact, although we are all cut from that self-same spiritual cloth, remember that there is more to our experience than our spiritual experience. Our experience makes us all very different in how we need to communicate with each other. With some people, we can be direct, open, and up front from the word "go." With many others, we need to communicate much more carefully, paying close attention to the inner hurts the person has suffered. Some people need to communicate with others a long time before revealing even the slightest bit of personal background. Some people cannot easily discuss emotionally charged issues such as abortion, politics, and religion because of previous attacks on their beliefs and experiences.

The good news is that "beneath" all the tough or jelly exteriors of people are individuals who want love, freedom, security, friendship, and loyalty.

> *People love their individuality, yet they need interconnection with others for fulfillment and long-term happiness.*

The interconnection that we seek with others is successfully accomplished through effective communication on many different levels. Sound complicated? It might, but thankfully it really isn't. Throughout this book you will be presented with many key ideas, insights, and simple tips to truly honor yourself and others . . . whether you are tough as nails or gentle as a lamb!

CHAPTER 3

Values:
The Key to Connecting
with Anyone!

ZIG ZIGLAR, ONE OF THE WORLD'S GREAT motivational speakers, once said, "People don't care how much you know until they know how much you care." I agree. People don't simply listen to people who are smart or have a breadth of knowledge in a specific area. People listen when they know how much you care. Having interviewed many people about what makes a person interesting and listenable, I have gathered that this point is not understood by most people. There is a common misunderstanding about what "caring" means. *Most people define caring, in part, as being unconditionally accepted by another person. People will not truly listen to us until we show them how much we care.* How can we show people that we are accepting of them and care about them?

1) *As you listen to other people talk, learn to see things from their point of view.* If you were in their shoes, how would you think? You don't have to agree with people to accept them as a person. You can respect their opinions and still disagree with them completely. You can show empathy without having to agree or compromise your beliefs or integrity: "You know, if I had been through what you have, I might think the exact same thing."

I recently had a session with a seventeen-year-old who was a member of a gang in Minneapolis. He had asked to see me because he heard that I was "cool." (Read that as someone anyone can trust.) He had worked thirty hours at his job to earn enough money to pay my session fee. I could have worked with him for free as a "kind gesture," but would he have been inclined to listen to any recommendations I had if he had seen me for free?

The young man had a problem. The gang he is in has only one exit door, and that is death. You either die of old age, or you die when you

41

leave the gang. Now this particular gang is structured like most gangs. The members are in a typical corporate pyramid structure where there is one CEO and many vice presidents, followed by many upper and middle management teams and then the largest number of employees performing various functions for the gang.

This gang heavily programs its members with the theme that they are family—and family takes care of family—and that you never do anything to hurt family in any way. Leaving the family is betrayal and grounds for death.

This was a lot for me to handle, even as a therapist. At one point I asked him to identify and explain some graffitti for me that he was doodling. He looked at me and shared with me some ambiguous information. I pursued my point and he simply said, "If I tell you that, I will have to kill you." He was straight faced and completely honest. I told him, "That's okay. I'm not that interested in art anyway."

He was about to make a move up into "upper management" on his eighteenth birthday. His eighteenth birthday would be the day that his fate would be sealed forever with the family. If he were in the gang as a legal adult, he could literally never leave. If he left now, he might be killed, but he might also figure out some technicality he could get out on, as seventeen-year-olds are not completely responsible in the gang. They are not yet in upper management. However, he was very concerned about leaving because every friend, every person he associated with, every human being he cared for and took care of and looked out after for the last eleven years of his life were in this gang.

I told him that it must be gut-wrenching to feel like he had to leave his family, the people he loves, in order to leave and try to make a life outside the family. I did not encourage him to leave or stay. I simply had him weigh the options. I presented various scenarios to get him to look at his potential in a post-gang life. He couldn't believe that I wasn't trying to get him to leave and even presented many good arguments for his staying.

"You are cool dude," he told me. "You are the first adult I've ever talked to who understood me. I'm going to figure out a way to leave the gang and get out. I've got a lot of stuff I have to do first, but thanks, Man. Really."

He stood up at the end of his two hours and extended his hand. He knows his identity, his exploits, and his experiences are safely kept by me from the world.

I created a safe place for him by taking his side and understanding his point of view and putting myself in his shoes. I experienced gang life from his side. I didn't let my opinions invade his experience. Everything he did that wasn't harmful to others I validated and sought more information about. I showed him many wonderful things he had done as a person both within the gang and independent of the gang.

It was a nerve-wracking experience, but one from which I learned a great deal. Never had my life been in quite that much peril. I left the session with what I learned, never to teach it or talk about it. He knew that what he said would stay safe with me. He could "feel" that I was "cool."

Be this way for people you love and care about and watch what happens. Be a safe haven for people and you will build rapport and gain the confidence of those around you.

2) Ask questions about the other person's beliefs and ideas in order to discover how they came to believe what they do. *As you ask questions of other people, use an attitude of curiosity and not one of contempt:* "I've never thought of it that way. How did you come to that conclusion?"

It is always amazing to me how people come to their beliefs and attitudes about everything from politics to religion to sexual mores. I recently had a lunch date with an old high school friend of mine, Susanne Lambert. We hadn't seen each other in nine years. The last time we saw each other was at a meeting to help get kids off drugs. This time was different. We ran into each other at my mom's funeral and promised to call each other and catch up. We finally did. We talked and talked. Finally, the subject got around to politics. Her Dad was a very conservative Republican, and I was a very liberal Democrat when we met in high school some twenty years ago. I told her that about ten years ago I gave up my Democratic shoes for those of the conservatives and she was floored.

"How could you do that?" she demanded. "The Republicans are a bunch of idiots. I am really disappointed in you!"

I couldn't believe it! I used to argue faithfully with her about how she should become a Democrat while she argued the other way!

"What got you to change?" I inquired.

"Oh, my dad had me brainwashed about Republicans. It's all I ever knew as a kid, and then I went out into the real world and found out that I wasn't a Republican. I was a Democrat."

She had switched her life-long belief, too!

What is interesting is that it is rare that people actually change their political and religious affiliations. In the United States, 71 percent of all adults will tell you what religious denomination they belong to, and it is invariably the same one they were in as six-year-olds. This is typical of political and social beliefs as well. We are generally reared in a certain fashion, and we rarely move from our original beliefs.

When you meet someone and you don't know how they came to believe what they believe, be sincerely interested and curious and completely non-judgmental and discover just how they came to believe what they do. You will learn that rarely do people consciously choose their beliefs. Those beliefs are programmed into the mind early in life. What's best is that your historical expedition into another person's mind will pay off in rapport points IF you do not criticize or show contempt for what the person has so freely disclosed to you.

3) *Discover a person's values,* and find out how they know when they have met their values so you can be not only a better communicator but develop a better relationship.

To discover a person's values we ask a few key questions:

"What's most important to you in life?"
"What's most important to you in a relationship?"
"What's most important to you in a friend?"

4) *Find out what these values mean to the person!* Having asked thousands of people this question,I have discovered a most interesting thing. Most people will not tell you their most important value until you've asked them two or three times. People tend to be very protective of what they hold dear, especially their values and beliefs. So, I always ask a follow up question:

"What else is important to you in life?" "What else?"
"What else is important to you in a relationship?" "What else?"
"What else is important to you in a friend?" "What else?"

Once you've discovered three or four values, you can learn what is really the most important thing to a person. If someone tells you that they regard love, happiness, health, and security as the most important things in life, you can then discover what really is number one in their life: "If you had to pick one of those four values that is the most important to you, which would it be?"

Imagine that the person tells you that health is the most important thing in life. Then you want to know what "health" means to that person. "How do you know when you have health?" The person may tell you that being healthy means a low body-fat percentage. He may say that health is the absence of illness. Or he might say that it is a feeling of vitality. Whatever he tells you is what that value means to him. *Now you know more about that person than if you had had simple small talk for weeks or months.*

Having shared his values and beliefs with you, the other person has disclosed what is most important to him. He has disclosed his soul to you, and most people disclose what is dear to them only to those they love and trust. Disclosure breeds trust, love, and respect. The very act of caring enough about another person to the point of truly understanding him shows your acceptance and respect. If you accept a person's values and respect those values, you build a bridge and create a powerful bond that makes it very easy for anyone to listen to your ideas, thoughts, and feelings.

People know that their values are very important to them. We live and die for those things and people we value. When you sincerely want to help people live up to their highest values, they tend to open up to you and bare their true soul to you more quickly than they would to anyone else. Acceptance of someone else's values is an act of unconditional love. Such love is sincerely appreciated.

The Four Types of Values

There are ends values and means values. Ends values are the emotional states, the feelings and inner experiences we ultimately want to enjoy. Happiness, love, joy, peace, serenity, passion, and ecstasy are all examples of ends values. Means values are things. They are things that can be physically touched and physically experienced. Means values are "things" like people, cars, travel, playing games, participating in sports, taking walks, owning possessions, and the like.

Means values often (but not always) help us attain ends values. In other words, traveling to some far-off destination (a means value) may help bring about peace of mind (an ends value).

There are two other kinds of values. These are moving toward values and moving away from values. We have been discussing moving toward values up to this point. Moving away from values include those things or states of mind that we do not wish to experience.

Some people do not want to be audited by the Internal Revenue Service. Therefore this is a moving away from means value. It is also the means to an end. People who don't want to be audited by the IRS might experience fear or anxiety as states of mind they are ultimately trying to avoid. Fear and anxiety are examples of away from ends values. You can't physically touch anxiety or fear, but you can definitely touch writing a big check to the IRS for back taxes. That's why the audit is a moving away from means value, and the fear it brings on is the moving away from ends value.

In order to more thoroughly understand the idea of values, both means and ends, moving toward and moving away, you can now participate in a set of unique self-discovery exercises. Understanding yourself is often a useful starting point in understanding other people. Carefully participate in the self discovery. What you want to look for is what you learn about yourself that is new.

In the spaces below, or in a journal or notebook, write the answer to the following questions. In this exercise, please use moving toward values only. (In other words, refrain from writing about what you do not want and what you are trying to avoid!)

Discover Your Moving Toward Values

1) What is most important to you in life?

2) How do you really know when you have it?

3) What else is important to you in life?

4) How do you really know when you have it?

5) What else is important to you in life?

6) How do you really know when you have it?

7) What else is important to you in life?

8) How do you really know when you have it?

9) Looking at numbers 1, 3, 5, and 7, decide which of these values is most important to you in life. In other words, if you could have only one, which would it be?

10) Looking at the remaining of 1, 3, 5, and 7, decide which of the remaining three values is most important to you in life. In other words, if you could have only one of the remaining three, which would it be?

11) Look at the remaining two values of 1, 3, 5, and 7. Decide which of these remaining two values is more important to you in life.

12) Write your four values below in the order you selected them as being most important to you.

My most important value in life is_____

My next most important value in life is_____

My next most important value in life is_____

My next most important value in life is_____

Go back to each of these four values and determine if they are all ends values. (Feelings, emotions, states of mind . . . things like love, happiness, security, freedom, God/spiritual life, etc.). If they are not, circle the values that are not ends values and then continue.

For each means value that you circled, what emotional state or state of mind does it create for you? For example, if you wrote money, what is it that money gives you? Does it give you freedom? Does it give you security? Joy? Happiness? Write down what state of mind or emotion the means value gives you next to the value in the twelve-step exercise above.

If you're like most people, you just learned some pretty interesting things about yourself. Isn't it funny how we can live in this body and experience our thoughts for all these years and still surprise ourselves about what is important to us? If we don't know ourselves as well as we thought we did, imagine how much less we know about the people we see and talk to every day. Please also consider that not only do we not know our spouses, our lovers, our children, our friends, or our co-workers, but neither do they know themselves as well as they think!

What this means to the communication process is that we often have two people who really don't know themselves as well as they thought they did talking to each other. Then misunderstandings occur, and arguments, fights, and all kinds of problems ensue.

One of the keys to being a great communicator is to really understand yourself and be able to rapidly gain an understanding of others.

Imagine that some of your friends might consider that the most important "things" in their lives means values. In other words, the most important values they have are their money, their house, their car, and their collection of antiques. How might this affect their daily thinking and communication? Is it possible that people who value objects have not yet considered what states of mind those objects bring them? Is it possible they have not yet considered other ways to get the same states of mind without the object?

Imagine that someone you like or care about is an alcoholic or a cigarette smoker. He or she craves cigarettes for some specific feeling. They "need" alcohol to experience some "state." What would happen if there was another way a person could experience those states without using artificial state inducers such as alcohol or cigarettes (or drugs of any kind)? People who need something to create certain states of mind with drugs or similar substances often experience communication difficulties because they normally find it difficult to share their experiences without the artificial state inducer present. Helping a person experience the states they have without the artificial state inducer can be an eye-opening experience for people, can't it?

CHAPTER 4

Building Rapport:
The Foundation of
Successful Communication

I REMEMBER THE DAY WELL. It was my first day as a public speaker. 1987. The subject was drug abuse prevention and the location was a high school in Minnesota. For years, Minnesota schools had been using a drug prevention program called DARE. This is a program that uses uniformed police officers to talk with children about the foolishness of using drugs. I had predicted in the early 1980s that DARE would not work and probably would actually cause kids to use drugs. Having been a child once, I remembered quite well that the experience of listening to a uniformed police officer could generate fear and it could generate compliance, but it definitely would generate rebellion. I shared my predictions, based on sociological principles, with school administrators all over the state of Minnesota. A few agreed but most did not.

I helped found an organization called Success Dynamics Foundation, whose goal was to get kids off drugs and alcohol and to stop other kids from starting in the first place. Our approach was apparently radical, and the resistance we received to our public point of view about the DARE program was substantial. Many heads were violently shaking yes or no, depending on whom you asked.

The facts added up, however. DARE failed to create long-term behavioral change in all the studies we could find. It simply didn't work and in some states actually seemed to have the opposite effect. How would we be different?

I walked into the school understanding quite well the principles of rapport. I knew how to use hypnosis with groups by utilizing certain communication patterns, and I knew what the students as a whole would believe about drugs, alcohol, and cigarette use. (Most kids used one or all regularly as seniors and still do at the turn of the millenium.)

I looked into the eyes of as many of the 1200 students as I could.

"Before we get started," I declared, "I want to tell you that I am NOT here to tell you to stop using drugs. I am not here to tell you to never start and I am not here to tell you to change in any way just because some guy walks into your school at an assembly and babbles endlessly about how bad drugs are. All we're going to do for the next period in this assembly is look at the various drugs, what they do, what they don't do, and how they might or might not affect someone's life.

"I used drugs and alcohol in the early 1980s," I told them. "I could never bring myself to smoke a cigarette. They just grossed me out they smelled so bad. Some of the experiences I had with drugs and alcohol were great and some of them were horrible. I want to tell you about one time when I had a great experience when I went drinking one night with some buddies."

Needless to say, my opening remarks completely freaked out the teachers and the administration. I could imagine that they were building the gallows in the band room and were just waiting for me to finish so they could hang me. I even questioned myself, praying my strategy was the right one for the right group! I told about a fun time a bunch of us seniors had when we went drinking. We got drunk, talked about religion, the meaning of life, and how important it was that we were all friends. I intentionally got in a good message on the drunk side, because when I came to the horrors of drugs, I was going to slam dunk every negative emotion I could and link those negative emotions to using or even thinking of drugs in the second half of my presentation.

I effectively had built rapport. The students were laughing and getting into my presentation. They couldn't believe I was there talking about a good time while drunk—and doing it on the school's money. I got them comfortable and the defenses went down. Then, when I had the group's attention, I went to work with the anti-drug message. It was powerful and profound and made a tremendous impact. I told stories about how a good friend of mine was busted during his first year in the military because one day he sold drugs. He was dishonorably discharged and never got a good job after that because of his one mistake. I told the story about how I almost died from a PCP overdose when I thought I was just smoking marijuana that I had bought from a friend. It was only the fourth or fifth time I had bought marijuana, but it was my last. I drove home stories of people who were maimed after drinking and driving. I pulled out every stop, and the vast majority of the students were in tears by the end of the presentation. I closed like this:

"My purpose today was to come and share the good and bad stuff that happens whenever we make a choice. I don't want you to quit smoking pot or quit getting drunk because of anything I said. I just want you to look at this stuff every day you take a drag on a joint or down some J.D. (whiskey). If you do that, it shows me that you were interested in what I had to say!"

Huge applause errupted. The teachers all looked dumbfounded. A few were applauding. Later I went to various classrooms and asked students what they thought of the presentation. And did they have any advice to make it better?

"Tell more stories of how people screwed up."

"You should have spent more time on what happens to the body when people smoke crack."

Only a few students said, "You didn't spend enough time on how good it feels to be high."

Whenever someone said something like that, I replied, "Good idea. It makes it more real if people know that this can be fun and that it doesn't always lead to death and disaster. Thanks!" I always validated every comment from every person.

Our program received national attention and most of it was good. We finally stopped our work in 1994 when it became politically incorrect to present information in schools the way we did. It was a shame, because we were making a difference. The lesson, of course, is simple: People want to be validated, and they want to feel comfortable while being honest with their feelings. If they know they can talk safely, they will disclose a great deal about themselves.

People want to be comfortable. Most people live in either personal or corporate environments that are either not conducive to loving communication or they are worse, often hostile and unkind. When people are in our presence, we want them to feel at ease. This sometimes means we have to do things we know will make people feel comfortable. Building rapport often entails doing and saying things that seem awkward but are perceived by others as loving and sensitive.

Most people enjoy talking about themselves and probably don't get to do it as often as they would like. This is one reason the values determination model is so important and effective. When you ask people about their values, you are asking them about their strongest feelings and thoughts. This is an important element in understanding people and can greatly assist in developing rapport.

Rapport is the perceived affinity between two or more people.

Become fascinated by what others can share with you.

Most people seem to try to be interesting when they should be interested. The truly authentic communicator is a curious soul. He or she wants to know more about other people. He or she is truly fascinated by what other people can share with them. You may sincerely wonder how you could be interested in some people. If what interests them doesn't interest you, then discover *how* they became interested in what they are interested in. In other words, if you don't like fishing, and someone you're communicating with does, find out how they became so excited about fishing. What experiences do they have that started this fascination?

In 1989 I went to visit my stepbrother, Chuck Welch, in Maine. I hadn't seen Chuck in years and I had no idea what to expect when we finally saw each other. Shortly after my wife and I arrived in Maine, Chuck said, "I've been tuna fishing for a couple of years now. It's hard work."

I remember wondering how hard could it be to catch a bunch of little fish in the ocean. You throw a net in, and you reel in a few thousand of those little buggers. Would I like to try it?

"Sure, let's go."

Chuck didn't live far from the ocean, and soon we were brought to a vehicle that looked like an ambulance without the logos, lights, and sirens. I was really going along for the ride and the special time to be with my long lost stepbrother. I didn't really care if I saw any little fish. Chuck opened the back of the ambulance-like vehicle and there lay a tuna.

"It's about 800 pounds. Pretty good sized, don't you think?"

My mouth about dropped from my jaw. "How does it fit in that tiny little can?"

I really said that! All the way over I kept thinking about how they would fit the little tuna into the little can, as in one per can. Then I saw this . . . monster! It was a whale, as far as I was concerned!

"How do you catch these things? You must have a huge ship to catch them!"

Chuck was off to the races with stories of how he signed on as a tuna fisherman, caught the fish, and how much each one was worth. He told me stories of how when you are deep sea fishing, you have to be careful of getting dolphins entangled in the nets, and how careful he is to make sure they are set free. I was fascinated!

When I got back to Minnesota, I went back to raising money for drug prevention programs for students all over the state. One day I went to talk to John Neumann, the owner of a Carbone's franchise in St. Paul. I remember it was just after my trip to Maine.

"Hi, Kevin," he greeted me. "Nice to see you again this year. Back for some more money?"

"Yep, I need to get a donation from you again this year. What have you been up to, John?"

"Been fishing a lot this summer. Working and fishing."

That's a pretty common theme in Minnesota. Working and fishing.

"Really? What do you fish for?"

"Walleyes, mostly."

"Ah . . ."

(As if I knew what a walleye was.)

"In fact, I caught some good-sized ones last weekend."

Having just returned from Maine, I thought I would take a chance and guess how big a walleye might be. I figured an 800-pound tuna came out of an ocean, and John was fishing on Minnesota lakes. So I went for 5 percent.

"What'd they weigh . . . about forty pounds?"

My question was sincere, but it took the wind out of John's sails.

"Well, no, Kevin. They were about four pounds each. I thought you knew something about fishing."

Nope, I don't, but I do know how to make an idiot of myself when I try to pretend I know something that I don't!

"No. In fact, I just got back from Maine, where my stepbrother was telling me stories about how he caught these 800-pound tuna . . ."

John cut me off.

"Well, Kevin, that's commercial deep-sea fishing. That's a whole different thing. Walleye fishing is something special."

John went on and on about his fishing experiences over the years. I learned an enormous amount about fishing in that conversation, enough to hold my own in future conversations because I asked lots and lots of questions. I asked about bait, hooks, how heavy the line is, what kind of equipment they use, and how they decide where to fish in which lake. I had never been on a fishing boat, but I now knew something about fishing for walleyes.

My lesson was simple. I could learn to talk with the best in a field if I were sincerely curious enough to ask the right questions! Today, when I don't know something, I say, *"I'm totally ignorant about that, but I'd be fascinated if you would explain it to me."*

> **By making others feel special, they will realize how special you are.**

One day I walked into the Barnes and Noble bookstore in the western suburbs of Chicago. It was a gorgeous Saturday and I was going to do a book signing. Of course, every author's fear is that it will be gorgeous day because then only a few customers will actually attend the book signing. There is something rather humbling about a book signing that no one comes to. This was that day.

My book *The Psychology of Persuasion* came out in mid-1996 and was met with a warm reception by the public as a whole. The book sold well and continues to do so because it is an easy to understand primer on persuasive communication. This particular Saturday would be quite different, however!

I sat at my table with my stack of twenty-two books and not a person in sight. I was disappointed, to say the least! I got up from hiding behind the stack, realizing that I didn't hold a candle to the first beautiful spring day of the year, and decided to meander around the store. Just as I was feeling as humbled as one can feel, I happened upon a young girl four or five years old in a wheelchair. By the way she was sitting, I suspected she suffered from severe cerebral palsy or multiple sclerosis. She couldn't talk. She was incapable of even making that beautiful little mouth move. Her mother came out from behind a stack of books and saw me bent down talking to the girl. (When I worked with elementary school kids, I learned that they love it when you get down on their eye level so they don't have to be face to face with your belt buckle.)

"My name is Kevin," I told her. "I saw you looking at me when I was over there sitting by myself. Was that you who was looking at me?"

She "nodded" her head.

"Is it okay if I sit here and talk to you for a minute? I'm kind of lonely and don't have anyone to talk to."

She "nodded" again.

"Thanks. Is that your mom up there?"

I pointed to her mother, and the little girl smiled and moved her head, indicating it was her mom. The little girl looked at my suit coat, which had a pin on it that said "SUCCESS."

"Were you looking at this?"

She moved her head indicating yes again.

"That's the word "success." It means that you do a good job at something."

I took the pin off and put it in her hand. She squeezed it.

"Can I put this on your dress?"

She moved her head, and I pinned it on her dress.

"Great. Now when you talk to your mother, you can tell her you are a success."

Her mother came over and knelt beside me.

"Thank you, Kevin," she said for her daughter.

"You have a beautiful daughter."

I looked at her face, smiling as her mother and I talked at her eye level.

"Thanks. She sure is. Your book signing didn't go too well today."

I looked at the little girl then back to the mother.

"Best one I've ever had."

I kissed the girl on the forehead, told her it was nice meeting her, and I was off to check out of the store and go to the next "book signing" of the day.

A few weeks later, my publicist, Lynda Moreau, sent me a letter from the consumer relations representative of the store. The store representative shared with Lynda the entire story of what had happened as the little girl's mother had shared it with the store rep. Lynda forwarded the letter to me, and it made my month.

Usually when you do something nice for someone, no one ever finds out. That is really the way it should be. I share the story here to underscore what you already know: No one knows how much you know until they know how much you care. I never learned the little girl's name, but I know I'll be looking up to her at the top!

You don't have to be able to talk to communicate. That beautiful little girl communicated with her eyes all I could ever want to "hear." She made my month with her smiles. Mastering communication skills is necessary for fulfilling your life's purpose, for creating authentic relationships, and for being happy. You will *always* need to be able to communicate effectively with people on all levels. The next time you see a little one that can't talk, maybe you can do the talking for them, on their eye level!

Your ability to build and maintain rapport in communication is one of the key skills of being a caring communicator. One of the great examples of rapport building in literature is found in the New Testament. You may remember the story of the Apostle Paul traveling to Athens, Greece. Athens at that time had a mostly pagan culture. The city was filled with idols and temples dedicated to mythological gods. As a Jew, Paul found that repugnant. Some of the local philosophers challenged Paul to a debate. They brought him to the infamous Mars Hill. It is here that we see Paul's ability to create rapport and touch people:

"Men of Athens, I perceive that in all things you are very religious." (This immediately breaks their skeptical pattern of thinking and creates an instant bridge for Paul to metaphorically walk on.)

". . . for as I was passing through and considering the objects of your worship, I even found an altar with the inscription: TO THE UNKNOWN GOD. Therefore, the One whom you worship without knowing, Him I proclaim to you." (Paul uses his rapport-building skills masterfully. The altar is one of the Greek objects of worship. The God he wants to discuss is one of the Greek gods. He is not going to talk about some new god!)

"God, who made the world and everything in it, since He is Lord of heaven and earth, does not dwell in temples made with hands." (God made the world, he tells them. He's obviously much too big to live in a human temple!)

Paul continues his discourse, explaining that God gives us life, our breath, and a place to live. He explains that God needs nothing from us.

". . . for Him we live and move and have our being, as also some of YOUR OWN POETS HAVE SAID, 'For we are also his offspring. . . . Therefore, since we are the offspring of God, we ought not to think that the Divine Nature is like gold or silver or stone, something shaped by art and man's devising."

Paul once again maintains rapport by returning to and citing Greek authorities. Building rapport is one step. Maintaining rapport and bridging into the message you wish to tell is another.

"Truly, these times of ignorance God overlooked, but now commands all men everywhere to repent, because He has appointed a day on which he will judge the world in righteousness by the man he has ordained. He has given assurance of this to all by raising him from the dead."

Paul has reached the crux of his message and has held the attention of his audience. It was the rapport that Paul built with the antagonistic philosophers that was the key to his successful communication here.

Rapport is much more than verbal compliments and praise, of course. It includes non-verbal behavior as well. Non-verbal behavior that enhances the building of rapport is detailed at length in my book *The Psychology of Persuasion*. A few important elements of non-verbal communication that build rapport are discussed below.

Non-Verbal Rapport-Building Skills

a) Physical Appearance. An individual's dress and grooming can help make someone feel either comfortable or out of place. How we dress in large part determines how much people will trust and like us. Each situation has a proper manner of dress affiliated with it. It seems like an inauthentic part of communication to dress in a certain manner to set people at ease, but indeed it is very authentic. You are dressing a certain way to help the people you communicate with feel comfortable. You have gone beyond your needs and desires of dress to that of others.

In 1982 I was a sophomore at the University of Wisconsin and was taking a class called "Nonverbal Communication." Half the grade in the class was to be based upon a paper each person would write after research in the field of non-verbal communication. The paper was like a mini-thesis. My idea was to see if how a person dresses would correlate to how rapidly he would get waited on in a retail environment.

I enlisted a friend to help me. What we did was play roles. I was the engaged bachelor who was looking for an engagement ring. He was my best man-to-be. We went to numerous jewelers all over the Minneapolis-St. Paul area. At half the stores we went to, we wore jean jackets, tee-shirts, and blue jeans. At the other half, we both wore coats and ties and dress shoes.

We measured the time it took for us to get waited on, and then we asked the value of the most expensive diamond the clerk could take out of the vault without calling a security person to be present while we were shown the ring.

When we were dressed in coats and ties, we were waited on almost three times as quickly as when we were dressed in jeans. When we asked to see the most expensive diamonds the store had available, we would see diamonds that were almost five times as expensive as when we wore jeans.

There was no question that how one dresses is directly related to the quality, comfort, and speed of service one receives.

b) Vocal Cues. It is best to gain rapport by matching the rate and tone of voice that your fellow communicator is using. It is not necessary to mimic the other person. Simply alter your speech patterns in the direction of the other person.

My personal tendency is to talk very quickly and make things happen at quite a speedy clip, especially in business. This speech-rate pattern works well for comedians, public speakers, and anyone who makes presentations before groups because the person can slow down if necessary (and it usually is appropriate to do just that regularly). Talking slowly and monotonously is a guaranteed method of losing the respect of your audience. Over the years as a public speaker and corporate trainer, I have learned that what works best is some variety. When discussing topics that are particularly serious, I will slow down and be more deliberate. When speaking about light issues or something that can be made light of, I will return to my normal pace, which is quite fast. Audiences have responded well to this formula and almost certainly will in the future.

c) Posture and Physiology. One of the most effective methods of gaining rapport is to match the posture and physiology of your partner. You sit or stand in a similar manner. This is called, "pacing." You can check later to see if you are actually in rapport by "leading." Leading means, for example, that if you are both sitting with uncrossed legs, you cross your legs. The other person will follow suit shortly, assuming you are in rapport. Once you have effectively led the other person, you can share your ideas and thoughts more constructively.

I was demonstrating this technique of pacing and leading in a public presentation some months ago. I asked a man from the audience to assist me in demonstrating rapport building to the rest of the audience.

After he was seated, I sat as he did and began to explain to the audience that I was intentionally slowing my breathing, sitting straighter, and crossing my arms because the gentleman was doing the same. I explained that it wouldn't be long before he would feel more comfortable and loosen up. I began asking him questions about his job, how long he had been there, and general questions about himself. I finally got him to open up with his comments about the recent elections, earnestly agreeing with his position. As soon as his head was nodding with mine about the good luck we had in the recent election, I immediately changed my body posture so that my arms were no longer crossed. He instantly did the same thing, and I immediately pointed out that I had led him as soon as I felt we had rapport. He confirmed that he felt comfortable with me when we were talking about politics and that he wasn't even aware that he had opened his arms.

He then returned to his chair and I asked another man to come up. This time I informed the participant that once he had attained a specific body position, he should keep it until we were done with the experiment.

He agreed to do so. He crossed one leg over the other, sat in a hunched posture, and breathed even more deeply than the man before him. I assumed a mirror position. I asked him about his work and his political views, which did not match mine in any way. We switched to sports and talked about the Minnesota Vikings and how close they came to the Super Bowl in 1998. I asked him why he thought they couldn't beat the Atlanta Falcons, and he began to give me his opinion. As soon as he was moving, I intentionally led him by opening up my body posture. His right arm twitched when he saw my left arm open up. Everyone in the first ten or so rows saw this and laughed. He didn't follow through but the point was clear. He was in rapport, and I had succeeded in leading him even though he didn't actually change his body posture. He wanted to!

d) Breathing. Watch how and where the other person is breathing from. You can pace the person's breathing pattern as a powerful mode to build rapport. People who breathe at the same rate are usually in sync with each other. When you make love with someone, for example, your breathing normally is matched breath for breath.

People sitting next to each other who watch a movie together will often breathe in sync with each other, especially if the movie is particularly dramatic or eerie. Certain emotions are likely to bring about certain breathing patterns, and these can be particularly useful to model if the opportunity arises!

All of these rapport builders lead us to an important key involving effective communication: *You must often be more like others than yourself if your goal is to engage people in deep and intimate relationships.*

Remember a time when you were in complete rapport with someone. This is a time that you both were almost thinking the same thing.

Were you sitting near each other?

Was your physiology similar?

Think of another time and answer the same questions.

When you experienced this moment of rapport with someone, did you feel that you were on a roll or experiencing enthusiasm or some other intense emotion at the time?

In the space below or in a personal journal, record your memories of a time when you felt very self-conscious about your body.

Write about a time when you felt very uncomfortable with another person or a group.

Using some of the information you have learned in this chapter, how might you have been more comfortable in this situation? Record your thoughts below or in a personal journal.

How Words Help Build or Destroy Rapport

Have you ever wondered what magical combination will really connect you with young people and inspire them to learn? Have you ever asked a teenager what he likes about a teacher? Ask your kids what they think makes a really great teacher. Remember your favorite teachers? What was it that you liked about them? If you are a teacher, a trainer, a parent, or an educator of any kind, you will probably be able to identify with Wendi's story in this section.

If you reflect back on your school years, you will remember very clearly those teachers that you simply couldn't stand! Those teachers will come to mind quickly because they made you feel small, stupid, not good enough, or embarrassed. The more you think about it, the more you will begin to find out what it is that those teachers had in common. They lacked the verbal-emotional skills to communicate with their students in a way that the students understood. They were unable to create a state of mind that would make a student receptive to what he was about to learn or experience. Unfortunately, these teachers either were not taught how to create a powerful and receptive learning state or they were unwilling to learn how.

Wendi Friesen relates a story of how ten minutes of rapport building (or not!) can frame how we feel about anything for a very long time:

> I recently went to a parents' night program at my son's high school. The parents were to spend ten minutes in each class as the teachers talked about what they would be teaching their students during the year. Now there is an easy job! Sheeesh.
>
> The interesting outcome for me was to note the way I felt for each ten-minute segment as a result of the communication and rapport (or lack or it) with each teacher. With each ten-minute segment, my state (the way my body and mind felt) would change dramatically according to the words that the teacher chose and the non-verbal communication that set the stage. So, for ten minutes I would feel excited and hopeful, then for another ten bored and disinterested, and for another ten curious. And so on.
>
> Each teacher had a choice of crafting words to delight and inspire, or to frustrate and confuse the parents! What was self evident was that these words and non-verbal communication would in large part determine the outcome for hundreds of students that year!
>
> At the first class, the leadership teacher walked into the room with his shoulders back, exuding confidence. (I am excited already!) He speaks clearly and looks each and every one of us in the eye. His words help me to be interested in what he is about to say. I want more. I want to go back to high school and be in that class! He tells us that he really cares about these kids, that there are some unique and fascinating kids in this class. He forces us to imagine the future as he tells us how other kids in leadership have used their skills to succeed. He talks about how it feels to be in leadership class. And he tells us how truly pleased he is to have our kids in his class. Wow!
>
> Next, I am off to science. I like science and I remember fondly my science classes from years past when I was able to bend glass in the Bunsen burner or dissect earthworms. (Really!) In the

ensuing ten minutes, however, the teacher managed to destroy any feelings of hope that I had.

She put me in a state of saddness, boredom, and frustration in less time than it takes to blow out a candle. She said that there will be some problems during the year. There are so many kids that they will have to share lab space, and that will make them frustrated. Some of this work is hard, she explained, and noted that the kids are going to have to work hard to grasp it. She said that it will be frustrating for them, and that it might also be frustrating for the parents. (I am not making this up.) I began to count how many times she used the word "frustrating." In less than ten minutes, she said it fourteen times. She took us right into the future, but it wasn't very hopeful. It was sure to be frustrating, with so many problems. She said she is a really tough grader. She doesn't like to give out A's. She won't accept late homework. But by that time it didn't matter, because all I wanted to do was get the heck out of there and go to physical education class. I was feeling a lot of empathy for my son for the time he was going to spend with this woman.

The same state that she created in the parents, she will create in the kids. My son got an 'F' in that class. No wonder. In one semester, a love of science was turned into boredom and frustration. By the way, she couldn't even pronounce the word "frustration" correctly. She left out the first "r," which frustrated me even further.

For two years I taught music at a private school. I had no teaching background, but I knew the power of my words and expectations and the state that they would create. As a teacher, I was a hit. Not because I am a great teacher, but because the words I used helped the students feel good about being there. One word in particular that these kids loved was "awesome." They told me that they never had a teacher who said "awesome." I wondered if that meant it was taboo to get excited about the little things. If these children were inspired by hearing the word "awesome," they were starved for good language.

The words are the thing, and for teachers, they hold the key. My students will remember me for not accepting their excuses, and for asking them to tell me what they could do, rather than what they could not do. These children will remember that whatever your mind tells your body, is pretty much what you are going to get. When a child would look at the music he was about to play and say, "I can't play that," the entire class would look at me for my reaction. They knew that when we tell ourselves we can't, then that is exactly what we get. My usual response to that statement was, "How do you know you can't?"

And that usually ended that.

But if the answer was "because it is too hard," then I would ask, "Is that what you want it be? Hard? Or would you like to make it easy? Because you can. Hard or easy is really your choice."

Several months into the year, the kids would study the new music, look up at me and smile, and say, "I can play that!" And then everyone smiled!

Teachers, and all the rest of us, have a choice about what kind of state a word or phrase is going to create. You can intend the same meaning with both of the following phrases:

"Since you don't know the information yet, it might be hard for you at first."

"As you understand the information, it will get much easier to grasp."

The first phrase appeals to the subconscious mind in a way that will create a negative state. It assumes this:

1. You don't know something.
2. It will be hard.

The second phrase assumes this:

1. That you will understand it, because it says, "As you understand . . ."

2. It will only get easier, and that you will grasp it as easy.

The phrases have the same technical meaning, but they don't create the same state. And the state (the way our mind and body feels from the words we use) is what will determine if we are receptive and open, or stumped and stupid.

Another example:

"This next segment might be hard. The kids last year couldn't get it right away, so don't worry if you don't understand it immediately."

"This next segment will be more challenging. You are a very sharp group this year, and since you communciate well together, I am sure you will find it easier than the group did last year."

The first phrase assumes that:
1. It will be hard.
2. There is proof based on results (of last year's class) that you won't get it.
3. You will worry and won't understand it right away.

The second phrase assumes that:
1. The work will be more challenging.
2. You are smart and communicate well.
3. That you will find it easier than those before you.

Once you realize that there are many ways to express the same message, you can discover many new ways to get what you want out of your students. Many of my students thought I was the best teacher in the whole wide world. I don't think I was a great teacher, but the kids felt good around me. I was just doing what I knew how to do—talk to them in words that create the feelings I want.

If you want your students or your kids to feel frustrated, worried, tense, or any other range of negative emotions, then use those words. And use them repeatedly. You can even use them to tell them not to feel that feeling. You could say "don't worry" hundreds of times, and the only effect it will get is to access a state of worry. That is the way our mind works. If you say "relax and trust yourself, and you will come up with the best solution," you will be a lot closer to creating a worry-free state in your student, your child, or yourself.

As a teacher, trainer, or parent, explore within yourself what is most important to you. What is the feeling that you want your students or your children to start the day or the class with? Take a moment to think about the way you start your day and what state it puts your students in. In one of my music courses I started every class with a magic trick. (Fortunately my own son kept me current on new magic tricks.) I think that the state it created was one of curiosity, intrigue, focus, attentive listening and watching. And that is a pretty good state to start any class.

Next, notice how you end the class. Do you leave students with a phrase that looms over them, such as "Don't forget, your essay is due tomorrow and if you don't complete it you will lose a half a grade"? If you leave them in a negative state, then that is the state they will associate with returning to your class the next day. You can still remind them of the assignments and consequences, and then do something to shift the state just before they leave. Make a joke, say something unexpected, get them curious. "And please remember to tickle your funny bone before class tomorrow." Or, "Also, for the test tomorrow, you will need to bring a No. 2 rainbow and a cloud with a silver lining." Catch them off guard, leave them wondering, curious, and interested in what you will say next.

Most of a student's day is much too predictable and too boring. When they hear the same things hour after hour, they begin to tune out. Teachers who lose the enthusiasm in their voices and drone on in a monotone will be tuned out. Teachers who use negative words and phrases will create an automatic state of heaviness and sadness simply by being in his or her presence. Find new ways to speak to the kids, new words that you are unaccustomed to using, phrases that will inspire them to feel differently. Learn one or two new phrases every day, and use them. Add a new phrase every day and allow student minds to grow and be more interested in what you have to say.

There are words that can create a favorable feeling when they precede a thought or an expression. Memorize them and then create more of your own. The part of the idea that is in italics below can be used for any subject, phrase, or sentence.

Phrases That Help Build Rapport and Bring about a Positive State of Mind

As you relax before the test . . .
(assumes you will be relaxed)

When you feel ready to write the essay . . .
(assumes you will feel ready)

The first thing you will notice when you know the answer . . .
(assumes you will know the answer and that you will notice it)

Imagine how good it will feel when you are all caught up . . .

As you understand the book it will get easier to write about . . .

Now look at some very simple ways to say the same thing, and create a positive mental state in your student. The first phrase is interpreted as negative by the subconscious mind. The second phrase sends the mind into a more receptive and positive state.

It won't *be too hard* to get it done this way . . .
It *will be easier* if you do it this way . . .

If *you can't do it right,* then don't turn it in . . .
When you do it the right way, *you will feel good* turning it in . . .

Don't run in the hall . . .
Walk slowly, please . . .

Don't *stop trying* to come up with the correct answer . . .
Keep thinking about it, and the correct answer *will come to you.*

Don't leave your homework where *you will forget it.*
Be sure to put your homework where *you will remember it.*

Now that you know how the mind works and how it interprets the words we speak, you will probably find many ways that you can improve your communication and many more ways to create phrases that ignite your students' minds.

As a fully indoctrinated soccer mom, I have the pleasure of having a son on a competitive team with coaches who speak positively to their players. These kids love soccer, love their coach, and they win. It wasn't always that way, and I will always remember a previous coach who spoke mostly in negative terms to the players. One of his phrases that stuck in my mind is an excellent example of confusing the mind and making it almost impossible to have a good outcome.

As the boys were running, kicking, and pushing hard to go faster, the coach would yell, "Don't stop running. . . . Don't stop running." On the one hand, the subconsicous mind hears the word "running," but then the conscious mind has the job of figuring out that what is really supposed to happen is to STOP RUNNING. But wait. That is not it, either. I am supposed to DON'T do that, so I am running—yes—stop—yes—and throw in don't, which is now a combination of DO and NOT, so now the boys, in all their huffing and puffing, must interpret a very complex message. DO (a positive) NOT (negative) STOP (negative) RUNNING (positive, which is what I was doing all along, but now am doing slower because my brain had to stop and figure out what the coach really means.) Wouldn't it have been a lot easier to say RUN . . . FAST?

We complicate our message in so many ways when there may be an easier, more elegant way to get the job done. Begin to notice what you are asking your students or athletes to accomplish. Notice if your message has been one that will create a bad feeling or a negative state, or will actually encourage them to forget something when what you really want is for them to remember.

> "Let's not make today another repeat of yesterday."
> > could be
> "Let's look forward to a new start today."

> "Don't get frustrated if you don't know the answer."
> > could be
> "Just relax and you know the answer will come to you."

Have you ever listened carefully to the words you and other people use in day-to-day communication? People tell you a great deal about themselves by the specific words they use. The tone of voice that one uses is very important in how the message will be received, but the exact words offer insights you will get nowhere else in the communication experience. Beginning today, start paying careful attention to the words and phrases people use that reveal their experience to you.

Imagine that you went to work, worked all day, and then came home. You were physically tired. How would you have described your experience to someone at home?

a) "I'm wiped out."
b) "I had a horrible day."
c) "I feel like I'm going to fall apart."
d) "I'm going to collapse."
e) "I feel dead tired."
f) "I'm sick of work."
g) "What a hell of a day."
h) "I'm completely exhausted."

Do these words create different images in your mind as you read them? They also mean very different things to those who say them. The words are labels for various internal representations. They are different for each person. Read each of the above statements carefully. Then do the following exercises:

Describe what image first comes to your mind when you hear the words "I'm going to collapse."

Describe the first images that come to your mind when you hear the words "I'm going to fall apart."

Notice that these two short sentences described the same experience to the person who said them, but they triggered very different images in *your* mind. When we hear people use metaphors and similes, we should clarify what specifically they are representing in their minds so we understand what they are saying and not what our representation of their experience is.

When someone says something and you have no idea what it *really* means, ask them, "What does that mean?" or "How do you mean?" You will be surprised how often you had a completely different picture of what is being discussed than what the sender was sharing with you. Your goal is to understand, not to interrogate. When a problem is more severe than is being suggested by communication, you can offer to assist. When a problem is certainly less severe than is being suggested by communication, you can offer to reframe the problem. Either way, you are now *really* understanding the people with whom you are communicating. Now, you can *really communicate* with them.

In the space below, write down common metaphors and similes that you hear in daily conversation. Some examples are given to help you get started. Think about the phrases that people at the office and in your family use regularly.

You can't always get what you want.
Life's a bitch.

Accidents happen.
It's hanging over my head.
I'm devastated.
You win some, you lose some.
Life is a game.
Life is a war.
Win at all costs.
It's not whether you win or lose, but how you play the game.
Three strikes and you're out.
That's life.
You never get a break.

Now, write the metaphors and similes you hear yourself and others saying day in and day out. Then predict how these phrases might shed light on what the person is really thinking.

We are all influenced by the people in our environment. Which of the metaphors in the list you made have you adopted into your communication? Write them below.

Which of the metaphors that you have adopted into your language are you finding useful in your communication? Write them below.

What do these metaphors mean to you? Write your definitions below.

Do others understand the meaning of these metaphors as clearly as you do? Why not?

What metaphors have you adopted into your language that you were not pleased with, but picked up by habit? Write them in the space below.

What does each of these metaphors mean to you? Write the definitions below.

Is the meaning of these metaphors as clear to those around you as they are to you?

In the space below, write how can you improve your communication so people understand you better.

What metaphors do you use that are more useful to your life, values, and beliefs? Use the examples below for ideas. Then write your own in the space below.
Examples:
Happiness is a day when I wake up.
Love makes the world go around.
Friends are forever.
Love is a journey.
Time is money.
Problems are puzzles.

Write your current life metaphors now.

What are some metaphors you can begin using to replace old metaphors that create limiting beliefs in your mind?

As you read the pages that follow, you will learn how to talk so everyone in your life listens. (Yes, even your parents AND your children will listen to you, too!) You will discover the simple communication secrets of the greatest love relationships, the most effective salespeople, the best talk show hosts, the most emotionally functional families, and more. You will become more comfortable and confident with people as they begin to listen to what you have to say.

CHAPTER 5

Communication 101: Skills for Success

He who has ears let him hear . . .
JESUS OF NAZARETH

Do You Want to Know the Answers to These Questions?

- How do you talk so people listen to what you have to say?
- How do you inspire people to consider your point of view?
- How do you encourage people in your life who currently ignore your ideas to suddenly reconsider you and take notice?
- If corporations are looking for people who can communicate first and learn their job second, what can you do to increase your value in the workplace?
- If communication problems are the major cause of divorce in our society, how can you assure yourself that you will communicate effectively with your partner?
- What simple things can you do so people will pay attention to what you have to say at home, in your family, at work, and even from the platform?

Communicating with People: The Basics

Communication is the most talked about and least understood element of human behavior. Our ability to communicate in so many physical modes (verbally, writing, computer, touch, etc.) is unparalleled in evolution and is uniquely human. The loss of one or two senses impairs communication but it doesn't stop us. Interestingly, effective communication is rarely taught at pre-high school levels. It is almost never taught as a basic skill in the primary grades when we need it most. To be sure, we learn vocabulary and spelling, but we don't learn how to express ourselves with our tone of voice to send the complete and proper message to our listeners. Most people never learn these skills, and those who do usually learn them in college where little if anything is retained for public life after school. If we can communicate effectively with people on an interpersonal level, we can eventually peel away the layers of the projected self and eventually get to the real soul at the center of the being. This chapter deals with the basics to help fulfill people's desire and ability to communicate.

Elements of Communication

Interpersonal communication at its most fundamental and basic level includes the following elements:

1) The Sender. The Sender is someone who wants to send a message to someone else. The message could be sent verbally or non-verbally.

2) The Receiver. The Receiver is someone who will be receiving a message from someone else.

3) The Message. In one form or another the Message is information.

4) Noise. Anything that causes interference in a message's true intent. Noise can delete portions of a message. Noise can cause information to be distorted or generalized. Noise alters the exact message from being replicated in the mind and soul of another person. Noise could include the sender's and the receiver's beliefs, attitudes, personalities, emotions, values, loud sounds in the background, or anything else that alters communication.

5) Feedback. Receivers and senders are both constantly sending feedback to non-verbal and verbal messages. Feedback is always a message, but by definition it is more specifically a response to another message.

6) Replication. The duplication of one sender's message in the receiver's mind is something that only people communicating at the level of talking to the soul completely succeed in. Short of that, it is an ideal or a goal of communication. We hope for as close a replication of the intended communication as possible.

7) Understanding. Understanding means the message as the receiver understands it.

Excellent communication is the ability to transmit a message by the sender to a receiver and have that message replicated in the receiver's mind. Excellent communication is receiving a transmitted message by the sender and replicating the message in the receiver's mind. If the receiver is uncertain about some aspect of a communication, it is the responsibility of the receiver to clarify the communication through the artful use of questions. The sending communicator also accepts the responsibility for the result of a communication. This means the sender must be certain to code each message so that it is received in a manner that is understandable to the receiver. Sounds easy enough, but is it really? All of this is of no consequence if a person is uncomfortable communicating with you in the first place.

Introduction to Interpersonal Communication: The Exercises

There are probably a few people whom you know that you find it easy to communicate with. These may be friends or family members with whom you have tremendous rapport, mutual respect, and many shared values. These exercises are not designed to help you with this tiny group of people. These exercises are designed to help you cope with the very difficult people in your life and on the job.

For each of these exercises you will need a partner to help you. Your partner should be someone who is also interested in creating excellence in relationships and improving his own intrapersonal communication. These exercises are all very difficult and teach you how to deal with the most difficult of communication problems. These exercises not only help you develop the skills to deal with difficult issues. They will help you deal with what we call "Well-Intentioned Dragons" in our lives that you will read about later. The first exercise is called Silent Eyes.

SILENT EYES: EXERCISE ONE

The purpose of Silent Eyes is to encourage eye contact and give your full attention to another person. Part of being authentic is giving full attention to someone. This is not as easy as you might guess!

Silent Eyes. Sit across from a person, being careful not to invade his intimate space. (Stay eighteen inches away, and no further away than four feet away.) For two minutes you must both sit in silence. Look at your partner for the entire two minutes. You succeed in this exercise if you are able to keep your eyes on your partner for the entire two minutes. It is NOT important that your partner maintain eye contact with you. It is only important for you to keep your eyes on your partner. If you even glance away for an instant you must begin again. After having successfully completed the Silent Eyes exercise, continue with the next exercise.

CLOSURE: EXERCISE TWO

The following exercise is called Closure. Closure teaches us a few important things about communication. In communication, we must be able to direct and follow. We must be able to give our full attention to others and "get out of ourselves." In other words, when someone asks us to do something, we should be able to do so without thinking about anything other than what we are being asked to do. Closure also teaches us the importance of closing each cycle of communication. Once someone has been kind enough to step outside of himself for our benefit, we should be able to sincerely thank him for being with us. Closure teaches us all this and more. It appears remarkably simple in its direction, but it is incredibly powerful when properly done.

Closure. Sit across from your partner at the same approximate distance you did in Silent Eyes. You will ask your partner to look at various objects in the room until you have reached a total of about twenty objects or locations. After your partner looks at each of these objects, you will say "thank you." Once your partner has looked at twenty objects, he will tell you that you have successfully accomplished this exercise.

INSTIGATION DEFLECTION: EXERCISE THREE

The next exercise opens us up to communicating with hostile people. People who are contemptuous are communicating from an intent to harm. Being on the receiving end of such communication is often very difficult. This exercise assists you in preparing for the worst in others. Many people may say mean things to you, intentionally or not, and most of us are not ready to handle this kind of hostility. Instigation Deflection vaccinates you against other people's negative conduct.

Instigation Deflection. Sit across from your partner at a distance similar to that of your previous exercise. However, move your chair about one foot to the left or right of where you were before to help create a different atmosphere for this exercise. In this exercise, you must give your partner permission to be hostile with you for two minutes. His goal, as difficult as it may be, is to be grossly unkind to you for two full minutes. He can try to hurt your feelings with words and actions. He has two minutes to go on a verbal rampage with you. He can say anything he wants. His objective is ultimately to get you to talk back, to disagree or to argue. He is instigating a fight. You succeed at this exercise when you have remained silent for two minutes and have maintained eye contact for the entire time. If you laugh or talk, you must begin again.

At the end of the two minutes, thank your partner and make sure he knows that this was YOUR exercise and that no harm was intended or taken. Hug your partner to erase any negative feelings that might remain. You asked your partner to do this exercise with you to help you become less emotionally upset by the unkindness of other people.

ANSWER MY QUESTION: EXERCISE FOUR

Your next exercise is called Answer My Question. The purpose of this exercise is to teach you how to be focused on the goal of your communication and your ability to ask the same question after it has been ignored or a new direction has been taken by your partner. Quite often in relationships we must address difficult issues in order for the relationship to grow. Many times, people, especially men, will try to change the subject without actually answering the question and resolving the problem. This exercise helps you gain the skill of staying on target.

Answer My Question. Move your chair away from where it previously was, but still facing your partner. You will now ask four specific questions, beginning with "Do dogs meow?" Your partner can answer in any way he wants. If he says "No," you can say "Thank you." However, your partner should at least temporarily choose not to respond, then change the subject and repeat the question, all instead of saying "No." Your partner MUST give you a "No" response before the fifth time you ask "Do Dogs Meow?"

You succeed only if you say "Do Dogs Meow?" after each incorrect response or non-response. The final three questions are:

"Are mailmen all women?"

"Do birds eat sharks?"

"Can you walk on water?"

The correct answer of course is "No" to all of these questions, and you must eventually elicit this response on or before the fifth asking. No time limit is necessary, but you should take no more than two minutes per question. You succeed if you only repeat your question in response to non-responsive answers.

Upon completion of this exercise, move your chair and sit directly across from your partner. The next exercise is called True and Kind Feelings. It's purpose is to reinforce the value of your partner after engaging in very difficult communication exercises designed to build your partner's communication skills.

TRUE AND KIND FEELINGS: EXERCISE FIVE

True and Kind Feelings. This final exercise must last a minimum of thirty seconds and no more than two minutes. Your partner must now tell you his true and kind feelings about you. He must tell you all those things he likes about you and they must be true. After your partner does this, then you must do the same.

These exercises teach you to communicate in difficult situations. After having mastered these difficult exercises, you will be ready for communicating with just about anyone about just about anything!

Intentional Communication: When You Talk on Purpose

When effectively participating in interpersonal communication, a key element on your part is that of Outcome-Based Thinking, or intentional communication. Outcome-Based Thinking entails knowing what your objective is before entering into significant communication with others. It is certainly not necessary to always have an outcome in mind, but there are many times when it is extremely important to know what direction your ship is headed. Sometimes it is nice just to "be" with someone. Other times it is nice to evolve, to share, and to create with others. Finally, we must learn how to compete and cooperate with others in an ethical fashion. Intentional communication teaches you how to do just that.

Outcome-Based Thinking can be utilized when you are problem solving in relationships or even when you are negotiating the price of your new home. Outcome-Based Thinking (OBT) is a skill that takes a little practice to master. You will get plenty of practice, however, as you will use OBT every time you want something or each time you need to enlist the cooperation of another person. When you are at work you may use OBT all day long.

What is this formula for success? How do you use OBT for effective thinking and effective communicating? Providing yourself with a road map that allows you to know where you are going is the first step. As noted earlier in this book, once you know where you are and where you are going, it's relatively easy to get there. The first principle in OBT is:

When you communicate, know what you want.

It is difficult to communicate effectively if you do not know what you want to communicate! Living a life that is multilevel in nature (physical, emotional, mental, spiritual) means that you are more cause in your life than you are an effect of other people's whims. You have more control. You are happier. You are empowering your life with a mission and purpose.

OBT starts at the macro level, and then works its way to the micro level. As you learn more about your true inner self, that part of you that is "most you," you gain a sense of purpose and meaning in life that you have not experienced before. On the smaller day-to-day experiences of living, *you use Outcome-Based Thinking to do what is in the best interests of yourself and all those around you.*

The exact process of OBT is detailed below. As an example, think of an upcoming appointment or meeting, one in which you are hoping to effectively communicate with someone in a one-on-one atmosphere. Once you have something specific in mind, integrate that situation into the OBT model below.

Outcome-Based Thinking
Model of Clear Communication

1) What precisely do I want out of the communication process or transaction?

2) What does the other person want? If I don't know, what are they likely to want?

3) What is the least I can accept in the process or transaction?

4) What problems could arise in the transaction or process?

5) How will I deal with each one, and if possible, use the problem as a BENEFIT for the other person?

6) How will I bring the process to a conclusion?

You can use this model of communication when you are negotiating the purchase of a new home. It's also simple enough that you can integrate the model into your daily life when you talk to your co-workers, friends, and lovers.

Excellence in communication on the interpersonal level often follows the discovery of just what others value in life and what their personal styles of communication are. In the next section of this chapter, you will learn more about the differences and quirks in people's behavior and communication that make communicating exciting and rewarding.

Understand the People You Talk to: Have You Ever Thought These Thoughts?

They won't listen to you if you aren't on their wavelength. If you don't understand some simple but important things about *them,* they will not be interested in what you have to say, no matter how much you talk.

They make no sense. *They* are incredibly annoying, and you'd give anything if you could just understand how they think and why they say the things they do. Why don't *they* just listen to me? Men think this about women, women think this way about men, and we all feel this way about our boss and our employees. You think this about your parents and about your kids.

We can talk so people will listen once we understand how other people think. Until we understand how people think and know what is important to them, we can't really communicate with them, can we?

Each woman is a unique blend of her genes, her life experience, her beliefs, her values, and her personality. Women think in a different manner than do men, generally speaking. Women have some different values and beliefs about communicating and about relationships than do men. In addition to this sometimes annoying fact of life, we all have roles that we play each day. When playing these roles we have specific values, beliefs, and personality traits that often differ significantly from our other roles. For example: A woman in the role of a lover experiences different values, beliefs, and behavioral tendencies than she does in her role as a mother or executive.

Fortunately we *are* all very different from each other. Part of life's journey is the continuous exploration and discovery of who you are and who those around you are. If you had the ability to completely understand someone with ease, there would be very little to share in a marriage or partnership of any kind. In short, once you understand someone completely, life would be incredibly boring with that person.

Another important part of life's journey is the continuous sharing of who you are and what you think with other people. You not only want people to listen to you, but you must have people listen to you in order for you to be emotionally healthy. Sharing your thoughts and feelings with others is very important. If you didn't have the ability to share your thoughts and feelings with other people, you would grow very sad. Once you begin to see that others will listen you, you begin to experience a growing sense of optimism and happiness about yourself and your life.

Understanding other people is something that is possible on many "levels." We can understand the basic differences in how men and women think. We can understand the basic personality types and how they think and communicate. We can understand the key behavioral tendencies of almost anyone in a short period of time and still have a lifetime of searching for the finer points that make us so wonderfully different from each other. By the time you are finished reading this book, you will have gained many insights about understanding other people. You will soon have more listeners than you ever thought possible, because you will have unlocked the secrets of talking so people listen. You will have the keys to setting people at ease and having them be open with you. By the way, the keys to talking so people listen are also the keys to building successful long-term relationships, should that be a goal of yours.

Beginning to Understand Others

Learning about the elements of powerful communication is synonymous with creating an open and safe environment for honest communication. This skill is something you will pick up easily as you continue to read through this chapter.

We learn many things in life by determining how something is like or different from something else. From a distance, flour looks somewhat like sugar, but upon closer examination the two couldn't be more different. We learn by smelling, tasting, touching, hearing, seeing, and thinking about all of the things we experience. We use our six senses. We learn by making generalizations about the things we experience. We learn by understanding the differences between things. Before going on to learn about how personality plays into your communication with others, answer these questions about yourself:

When you talk, are you talking on the same channel as your listener?

How are people perceiving you in your various roles?

Is that how you want them to perceive you?

Do people think you are one way, and you are constantly trying to get rid of the label you have been stuck with?

There are six billion people on earth, each remarkably unique. An aerial photograph taken above a football stadium shows 100,000 people watching an event. They all appear to be pretty similar at a distance. As we move in closer, the people look different from each other. They act differently from each other. They are different from each other. As you begin to look at the other people around you, we will start from a distance and see how people are like other people. As we move in closer, we will learn the finer points of how they are different from each other. The similarities you discover in others will help you gain a rapid basic understanding of how they think and how you can talk to them. As you discover the differences, you will become skilled at communicating with almost all people in almost all situations. The best part is that you will be comfortable in doing so.

Closure in Communication: The Power of Goodbye

The ability to close, politely and effectively, a cycle of communication is a skill that more people need to become adept at. Closure is the ability to acknowledge the other person, to say "Thank you" to the other person, or to confirm that what was said was understood. Closure is the final step in any segment or cycle of communication. You have no doubt been on both ends of a communication that "didn't end." Someone you cared about may have walked out of a room, hung up the phone, or switched subjects in mid-conversation without explaining why.

When cycles of communication are not completed, it leaves a person with tremendous frustration and often anger. You can always be certain to have closure in communication by acknowledging that you have heard and understood what a person has said to you. It is not necessary to agree with someone if you are not prepared to. It is necessary to close each cycle of communication.

Think of a time when someone hung up the phone without saying goodbye.

How did you feel?

Think of a time when you gave someone a gift and they did not express appreciation, gratitude, or even a simple "thank you."
How did you feel?

Why do you think closure is important to you in communication?

What specific things can you do to be certain you close all of your cycles of communication with acknowledgment of some kind?

Growing in skill as a communicator helps you forge long-term relationships. It helps you fulfill your life purpose and mission. Utilize the information you have learned in this chapter. If you want to be an outstanding and authentic communicator, go one step further.

Do You Enjoy Being with People Who Want You to Change for Them?

I recently accepted a client whose presenting issue was that he wanted to meet and eventually marry someone who was "exactly like me in my religious and political beliefs." We spent our first session discovering that there were only two churches of his specific denomination in the entire state of Minnesota and that there were only seven unmarried women, including women who were forty years his senior, in the two congregations. I suggested that he might be interested in meeting other women and accepting them for their differences and learn to honor those differences and possibly learn from those differences more about himself.

"If I married someone whose beliefs were different from mine, they would have to change to believe what I believe," he responded.

This was not what I was hoping to hear.

"What would happen if she believed some of the things that you do, but not all of the things that you do?"

"Then she would have to change and believe like I do or else I just couldn't be with her."

When he refused to allow someone into his life that wasn't a blueprint of his own religious beliefs, I decided to terminate our sessions. Asking someone to change for you is a sure recipe for failure, as we all know. Your experience is just like mine here, isn't it?

> *If you try to change people, they will resent you. Avoid the temptation!*

We can all change and improve ourselves. Change is healthy and good for us. What isn't so useful is demanding that others change for us. People need to be accepted and allowed to change of their own free will. Most people tend to strongly resist those who want us to change to fit their image. We may have to tolerate those who want to change us, but we won't listen to them. We won't truly care about what they have to say. It's okay to make changes within yourself, but except in rare circumstances don't try to change the behavior, attitudes, and habits of other adults.

Many parents "care" about their children, but it is not always apparent to the children (whether they are now full-grown adults or toddlers!) that they are accepted. When people know that you accept them, then they are more likely to perceive that you care about them.

> *If you accept people for who they are without demanding change from them, you are likely to gain their ear and respect!*

A Primer of Acceptance

One leader who cared for and accepted the common person without demanding personality changes was Jesus of Nazareth. He did not appeal to the leaders of his time but to the masses of the people of his country. He accepted sinners, women, and children and gave an open invitation to all three of these groups to spend time with him and to listen to him speak. These people listened to Jesus because he accepted them. He asked for their ear, and they gave him their respect.

For centuries the prophets of the God of Israel would bring their messages and words of warning to the kings of Israel and Judah. When they came to the crux of the message, these messengers would underscore what they were about to proclaim with the phrase, "He who has ears let him hear." Later, as Israel became an older nation, Jesus would regularly highlight his sermons with the echo of prophets past. Jesus knew how to talk so people would listen.

Jesus was not a great communicator merely because he could make a profound statement. Jesus was a great communicator because he was brief and to the point. There is no recorded speech that he gave that lasted more than fifteen minutes. Imagine that!

> *Jesus knew that to be brief meant he could be profound and his message would not be lost in oratory. He made his point and sat down!*

Jesus was a master at the artful use of questions. He rarely answered questions (especially from his detractors) with a direct answer. Instead, he would respond with a question of his own to begin a thought process in the mind of the inquisitor and more importantly to be in control of each communication. Jesus knew that *he who asks the questions has the power and control to take any conversation where the speaker wants to go with it.*

> *Ask questions to gently direct your conversations with others where you want them to go!*

Jesus was also a master storyteller. He would often share his ideas in easy-to-understand metaphors or complicated riddles, depending on the audience. *His stories were always short and nearly always controversial. His habit of being politically incorrect made just about everything he had to say memorable.*

Model Great Communicators Who Talked Their Way to the Top

The great communicators of the world have always found that their leadership skills are simply an extension of their ability to communicate remarkably well. Many of the world's great communicators have stories to tell of how they overcame adversity to make it to the top.

Each of us has been through many challenges in life, and we have all developed resistance to people around us. This is both good and bad in many respects. The good part is that the resistance is like a vaccination at times. Eventually, we understand that some people are just unkind and what they say has no bearing on our value as people. Unfortunately, this same resistance can also make communicating particularly difficult.

You have been yearning to share ideas and thoughts with many people but they have repelled you. On one level, you are drawn to them and they to you. On another level, they just don't listen, regardless of your intentions.

You already know that you can be "open and honest" with some people, "calling a spade, a spade." With other people who are "sensitive," this straightforward "honesty" can be very hurtful and appear unkind, regardless of intention. Therefore you will need to discover how direct or indirect your communication must be with each person you meet. Most people will recognize when they are being manipulated. But when you act in another person's best interests, your message is likely to eventually be accepted in the way you intended it.

By using the skills you have already learned, you will be able to develop specific strategies and communication techniques to help another person pay attention to you and seriously consider your feelings and ideas. You will be soon be able to effectively communicate your feelings, ideas, thoughts, and suggestions to those around you and gain a new respect from the people with whom you come in contact. We need to understand how to effectively communicate in order to peel through the layers of the onion to get to the center, the core, the soul. If your current state were that of energy, there would be no layers to peel!

The Great Communicators

It seems obvious that in a book about utilizing communication skills to achieve excellence in life we would look at the world's all-time great communicators. The question arises, how did the greatest communicators in history got their points across to their audiences? You will learn how to master the same communication skills they used. In short, people will soon find you more charismatic, more interesting, more thoughtful. And they will listen to you. This is the first lesson in peeling the layers to get to the soul. This outer layer is the hardened and very human physical layer of communication.

Remember the old E.F. Hutton commercials on television? Before the days of the discount broker and internet stock trading, E.F. Hutton was the leader in marketing financial advice, largely because of the company's creatively brilliant commercials.

"My broker is E.F. Hutton," someone says, and everyone else in earshot falls silent. Then the narrator intones, "When E.F. Hutton talks, people listen."

From this moment on when you talk, people will begin to listen. But not because of the great financial advice you are about to offer! People will listen because of the new respect you have for them and their true self. Imagine how people will feel if at the non-verbal and unconscious level they "feel" you connecting with them in ways that very few ever have in the past!

When you think of people who knew how to touch the hearts and minds of people, your mind immediately goes to the great speakers and leaders, doesn't it? Abraham Lincoln, Martin Luther King, John Kennedy, Jesus of Nazareth all come to mind, don't they? Of course, you don't have to be a world-changing leader to be on the same wavelength as other people.

Think of some contemporary communicators who are exceptional at capturing people's attention. What do you think of Larry King, Oprah Winfrey, Geraldo Rivera, Barbara Walters, Jane Pauley, Tom Brokaw, Dan Rather, Ed Bradley, Tony Robbins, Zig Ziglar, Bill Clinton, and Ronald Reagan? Most people have strong opinions about all of these individuals, but they still share one characteristic: When they talk, people really do listen.

In your own circle of friends, family, and co-workers, you discover that some people have gained the ear and respect of others. Many people in these groups are merely tolerated by others. Where do you fit in? What is the difference between those who are listened to and those who are not?

Respecting other people and accepting them without judgment will be a key to your becoming an outstanding communicator. You needn't be articulate or particularly intelligent to be a great communicator. You need to be able to share without need of reciprocity (their giving back to you) with other people. When you can let go of your need to "get" something out of people, you will lower their unconscious defenses and get closer to the heart, the soul, them, who they are.

Do You Have to Be Politically Correct
to Connect with People?

Some 1800 years after the death of Jesus, Abraham Lincoln would become yet another politically incorrect leader who had a knack for being controversial, memorable, and listened to. In a day when speeches of one or two hours by political figures were not uncommon, Lincoln gave his most famous speech, the Gettysburg Address, in less than five minutes. "Four score and seven years ago, our fathers brought forth on this continent a new nation, dedicated . . ." Lincoln knew the secrets of talking so people would listen. Like Jesus, Lincoln invited the common man to the White House to discuss any issues they wished on certain days. He wanted to stay in touch with the pulse of the nation and was one of the last presidents to do so. *People listened to him, in part, because he listened to them.*

No, you don't have to be politically correct for people to listen to you. Those you communicate with simply need to know that you care for and respect them.

Give People a Dream—Something to Live Up to

John F. Kennedy, another great American president, is remembered for his ability to get people to listen. He gained the respect of Americans by appealing to citizens as a collective group of people, as a team. "Ask not what your country can do for you, but ask what you can do for your country," he declared. Those words echo through the decades and are as loud today in the new millennium as they were nearly four decades ago. Kennedy made America greater than the sum of its parts, its people. When Kennedy made it a goal to put a man on the moon by the end of the decade, many people laughed. But they listened, and in July of 1969, seven years after Kennedy's death, that impossible dream was realized because he talked and people listened. When Kennedy spoke, *he made people feel important and part of something bigger than themselves.* He was a unifying force in history.

Help people see they are part of something bigger than themselves!

In the late 1960s, another great American leader gained the ear of a nation. This great man gained the ear of the nation as he shared his vision of America. "I have a dream that one day . . ." Martin Luther King spoke of black and white standing side by side, building a greater nation, greater than the sum of its parts. He appealed not only to black citizens, but to the nation as a whole, emphasizing that civil rights and freedom are inalienable rights of all Americans. He changed the face of America because *he helped people see a believable and attractive future that his listeners could have a hand in shaping.*

Help people create a believable future that your listener can really help shape and make real!

Be Willing to Disclose to Foster Authentic Communication

By the beginning of the twenty-first century, women had begun to emerge as major powerbrokers in America. One woman in particular, Oprah Winfrey, became someone to whom people listened. *She succeeded where others failed as communicators because she was willing to disclose something about herself before asking others to disclose their innermost thoughts.* It is common knowledge that Oprah's life has had many great challenges, and we all know of her public battle with and victory over obesity. In 1998 one television show she hosted implied that beef was not edible, and that very day millions of Americans stopped buying beef! When Oprah has an author on her show, the author becomes an overnight success, selling tens of thousands of books. When Oprah talks, America listens. She has shared with us her problems, and now she asks others to share with us their problems. Oprah Winfrey has become the most financially successful self-made woman in American history.

It's rarely a good idea to monopolize a conversation by endlessly rambling on about yourself. It is a good idea to disclose tidbits about yourself to foster communication with other people. Most of us won't be willing to share our most embarrassing moments if others don't share theirs, too! If you want to be recognized as a genuinely charismatic and powerful communicator, you can feel free to reveal little failings and weaknesses about yourself.

It always makes sense to reveal an obvious weakness about yourself to others because someone else will find your weaknesses and reveal them for you if you don't! A little self disclosure goes a long way toward building rapport and trust as a communicator.

Be willing to disclose a little about yourself to generate trust in your relationships.

All of the people you have read about on the preceding pages were able to get other people to listen to what they had to say. Each succeeded in specific areas of communication. Lincoln was not a great orator, but he excelled at having his finger on the pulse of a nation. He listened before he spoke. Oprah Winfrey disclosed her personal challenges and life problems in front of a nation, and America embraced her, making her the most listened-to woman in the world.

CHAPTER 6

Understanding Personality Traits

IN THE FIELD OF PSYCHOLOGY, there are many assessment tools to help us understand what personality types certain people are and how best to communicate with them. A test called the Myers Briggs Type Indicator is one of my favorite tools for learning how people experience their life. Understanding someone's "true" personality would make it very easy for you to communicate with them. Unfortunately, we can't give everyone we meet a time-consuming test, so we will consider a simple strategy of quickly understanding others so we can talk to them on their wavelength. When you talk on someone else's wavelength, you help them to be more at ease with you, thus peeling off their layers of decades of defensive communication behaviors.

Let's consider two significant behavioral tendencies that greatly influence how we will communicate with those around us. Later in this book you will learn many more key behavioral tendencies that will help you communicate effectively with others. For now, use yourself as an example as you look at these two tendencies.

Do You Lean Toward Being More
Introverted or Extroverted?

First, you probably tend to be an extrovert (outgoing) or an introvert (more reserved).

Extroverts make up about two-thirds of the adult population in English-speaking countries. People who tend to be extroverted normally get their batteries charged when they are with other people having fun. Introverts tend to get their energy from being alone or involved in activities they can do by themselves. Introverts particularly like time to think, "to be inside of their heads," and they tend to be idea people.

Extroverts tend to have a large number of friends. They tend to enjoy being part of a team and like interaction. Extroverts are easily distracted and generally have many irons in the fire. Extroverts are "take action now" people. They will jump in head first, often before they look at what they are jumping into! Introverts tend to have fewer but closer friends. At work they normally prefer to have a project they can call their own. They don't necessarily need to work by themselves, but they do like to be able to delve into their work without the constant input of others. Introverts can single-mindedly work on one project at a time or one facet of a project at a time and be very happy doing so. Introverts normally like to evaluate their decisions as to what they will do on a project. They like to look before they leap.

Are You More of a Thinker or a Feeler?

Second, you probably tend to be either a Thinker or a Feeler in your thinking processes.

A Thinker will do the logical thing. A Thinker likes to evaluate a situation, size up a problem, and consider all the facts. The process may be slow or fast, but he likes to consider information. A Feeler is a person who would more often prefer to go with his gut instinct. He may know what he wants to do very quickly, or it may take time, but he prefers not to evaluate as much information. He will make his decisions based on how he feels.

A Thinker is often described as analytical or calculating. The Thinker will tend to be honest, even if being honest hurts a person's feelings. A Feeler tends to be described as empathetic and sensitive. The Feeler would rather be indirect or tell a white lie and spare the feelings of another person. The Feeler is very aware of people's sensitivities and does not want to hurt anyone's feelings.

About two-thirds of men are Thinkers and about two-thirds of women are Feelers. Decide where you might tend to fall and then continue.

Look at the graph below and see where you would "line up" on the graph. Think about various individuals you know.

- Who do you know who tends to be very emotional in their talk and thinking?
- Who do you know who tends to be very logical in their talk and thinking?
- Who do you know who tends to be very extroverted?
- Who do you know who tends to be very introverted?

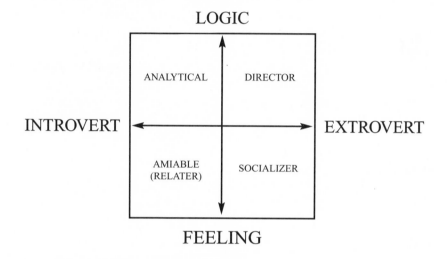

The Personality Type Graph above outlines four personality types people tend to gravitate toward. Carl Jung introduced the groundbreaking work of personality typing in the middle of the twentieth century. Today we have gone far beyond Jung's original work. In this book, we hope to provide a thumbnail sketch of the four basic patterns of behavior and communication that emerge from our living after birth. When you know which basic personality type your listener is, it is much easier to talk so he is comfortable with you. When two people are the same personality type, we say they are on the same channel. When one person is not the same personality type as another but communicates to that person in his or her personality style, he is also on the same channel. This is a fundamental key of peeling the layer of the onion. *Be with people where they are.*

Communicating with People Using the
Four Basic Personality Styles

THE ANALYTICAL (THINKER) PERSONALITY

The Thinker personality is someone who tends to be withdrawn and very rational. The Analytical Thinker is someone who enjoys (or is good at) solving problems. He tends to be good when using numbers. He makes decisions slowly and generally wants plenty of details about any idea, proposal, or purchase. The Thinker is slow to action. He likes facts and figures. The Thinker personality normally considers it a weakness to show or express too much emotion. The Thinker respects intelligence, logic, and rational thinkers. Many accountants, engineers, and computer programmers are analytical personality types.

They listen to people who have obviously considered all the facts about something and are not speaking emotionally. The Analytical Thinker is interested in listening to people who have thought out a problem or difficulty before bringing it up in conversation. They do not respect emotional outbursts.

HOW TO IDENTIFY AN ANALYTICAL (THINKER)

Thinkers tend to be well groomed and meticulous dressers. They are very organized. The Thinker tends to follow the rules to the nth degree and insists that others do so as well. The Thinker personality is one who can be very compassionate with others. Thinkers often make unkind remarks about themselves and how they fail to measure up in some way or another. The Thinker wants things and people to be perfect. He often gains control in interpersonal relationships by threatening to become angry. The Thinker sincerely appreciates support from others and the ability to be alone at times.

Analytical (Thinker) personality types look at us while we are talking to them and say to themselves:

Is what this person is saying making any sense or is he just babbling on?

Has this person considered the facts of the matter?

When they say they know, do they really know, or just have a feeling?

continued

> *Doesn't it seem reasonable that people act with too much haste before making careful decisions?*
>
> *What elements and data go into determining whether this is a logical proposition?*
>
> *How can a person evaluate the significance of a relationship after one night out on the town? Sure, it was fun, but life is about a lot more than fun.*
>
> *The truly sharp person analyzes his options, then steps back and evaluates those options.*

When you are talking to the analytical person, there are certain key words and phrases that tend to create and develop rapport with them. Words that really help you get on the Thinker's wavelength are listed below:

Rational	Frugal
Logical	Analyze
Sensible	Equation
Focused	Bottom Line
Attention	Dollars and Sense
Careful	Reasonable
Detail	Intellect
Consider	Statistically Speaking
Calculate	All Things Considered
Evaluate	Comparing Apple and Oranges
Measured	Weighed Carefully
Value	Useful
Compare Apples to Apples	

Talk like this when you talk to a person whom you believe to be an Analytical (Thinker):

"Don't you think kids should really pay more attention to detail *when they are doing their homework?"*

"Doesn't it just make sense *that people should make* rational decisions *about what they buy instead of being so impulsive?"*

"When I go shopping I buy products that are a good value *and reasonably* priced."

THE RELATER PERSONALITY

The Relater is a person who is quiet and thinks with his emotions. The Relater is normally a soft-spoken person who seems to care about other people's feelings. He also cares about his own feelings and tends to be sensitive. The Relater is someone who is slow to make decisions and normally seeks the approval of others before making decisions or purchases. Relaters love to take care of other people and they hope you appreciate them for their caring. Relaters are good caregivers and can often be found in therapeutic fields of all kinds. The Relater wants everything to be okay with everyone. They want to avoid stressful situations as much as possible and they sincerely appreciate the respect of others. The Relater will attempt to gain control by putting off projects or issues until later.

Some words that help you get on the same wavelength as the Relater are listed below.

Kind	Gentle
Nice	Love
Happy	Share
Concern	Touch
Feel	Nurture
Quiet	Care
Satisfied	Diplomatic
Consistent	Listen

The Relater will listen to people when they know that you are concerned about their feelings and the feelings of others. The amiable does not listen to people who hurt other people's feelings. They are offended easily and are careful not to offend others when talking.

HOW TO IDENTIFY A RELATER

The Relater is a person who tends to be very laid back and casual. He tends to talk of avoiding confrontation and hostile situations. Relaters tend to speak quietly and with a gentle and indirect manner. This person does not like to make the decisions and will encourage others to do so or simply go along with the crowd.

> **Relaters look at us while we are talking to them and say to themselves:**
>
> *"Does this person realize how much he is hurting my feelings?"*
> *"Can he talk a little quieter?"*
> *"Why is she always in such a rush when she talks with me?"*
> *"I like the way she asks me what I want to do even though it really doesn't matter. She's nice."*
> *"How can they make decisions so fast? Shouldn't she take her time and just think about it?"*

> **How to talk to a Relater:**
>
> *"Isn't it nice when people actually ask what you would like to do before racing off and deciding without you?"*
> *"Isn't it nice to actually be somewhere where there isn't a lot of noise?"*
> *"I'm wondering how you would feel about spending a quiet evening with me."*

THE SOCIALIZER PERSONALITY TYPE

The Socializer is a person who thrives on interpersonal communication. He loves to engage people in conversation. The Socializer is someone who can stay up all night talking. The Socializer is a person who will throw parties, organize group functions, and be the life of the party. The Socializer is offended when you leave after visiting only three or four hours. The Socializer wants to have fun and develop relationships. The Socializer is fairly quick to make decisions, although he tends to seek the advice of others before making purchases. The extreme Socializer (furthest away from the center on the graph) will talk with a great deal of verbosity and also speak quickly. Socializers sometimes forget to listen to other people as they are very often wrapped up in all the things they want to share with you. Socializers can talk about the same subject for hours without getting bored. Socializers can hurt the feelings of others without being aware of it as they often speak what they are feeling and often do not censure their communication. The Socializer works hard to gain your approval and acceptance, so validate this person. The Socializer gains control of situations through charm and charisma.

The Socializer will listen to you when he knows you are enjoying listening to him. He will often be very supportive of what you have to say and agree with you if you are passionate enough about your point of view. The Socializer expects you to listen to him first before he listens to you.

Some words that help you get on the same wavelength as the Socializer are listed below.

Fun	Energy
Spirit	Happy
Enjoy	Activity
Party	Event
Talk	Love
Flow	Go
Cheerful	Excited
Playful	Optimistic

HOW TO IDENTIFY THE SOCIALIZER

Socializers are people who feel uncomfortable when not talking. Socializers are in their element when people are having fun. They prefer not talking about subjects that are philosophically based, at least not in public functions. The Socializer is very much driven by the things and people around him. A majority of Socializers are women. They tend to make decisions with their feelings and not necessarily a calculation of facts.

Socializers look at us while we are talking to them and say to themselves:

"Why can't you just loosen up and have some fun?"

"Where is it written that work has to be stressful and dull? Work can be enjoyable."

"You don't have to overanalyze everything, you know."

Communicate like this when you talk to a socializer:

"How would you like to go out somewhere where there are lots of people and just have some fun?"

"Would you be interested in hosting a party?"

"If I take care of the details, will you greet the people?"

THE LEADER PERSONALITY TYPE

The Leader is someone who is in charge and makes quick decisions. He tends to think emotionally and be very up front with people. The Leader communicates with less verbiage than does the Socializer, but like the Socializer can hurt other people's feelings. The Leader is someone who is focused on results. He wants the job done and he wants it done yesterday. Leaders think logically and quickly. They make a lot of decisions and although they do not like to make mistakes, when you make as many decisions as they do, it goes with the territory. Leaders tend to be big picture people, leaving details to the analyticals that work for them. Most upper-level CEOs and entrepreneurs are Leaders. In family settings, parents tend to take a director role by default. Men tend to make up the larger portion of directors, contrasting the Socializer personality type made up by more women. Leaders prefer brief communication with everyone except those they are closest to in business and in personal life. Leaders tend to be quick to judge.

If you want a Leader to listen to you, you must prepare your communication with the Leader in advance to be brief, accurate, and to the point. What you say should have immediate and obvious practical value to the Leader if he is going to engage you in conversation. The Leader will listen to you if you acknowledge and understand his time constraints.

Some words that will help you get on the Leader's wavelength are listed below.

Results	Success
Fast	Decide
Achieve	Brief
General	Big Picture
On Time	In Time
Concise	Effective
Adventure	Persuade
Sure	Independent

HOW TO IDENTIFY THE LEADER

The Leader isn't necessarily the center of attention at the party, but he usually is sought after. His confidence and the air about him definitely reveal a sense of his being in charge. The Leader is someone who will likely walk and talk quickly. He likes his trivial conversations to be very short paced and will go into greater detail with people he respects and likes.

What the Leader is thinking when you are talking to him:

"Be brief and to the point please. I'll ask you questions if I have any."
"If you got to the point quicker I might say yes."
"After two minutes I'll be thinking about something other than what you are saying."
"When you work as hard as I do then you can complain."

Communicate like this to a Leader:

"I only have a couple of minutes . . ."
"What is most important to you in . . ."
"I've got an idea but I don't have a lot of time to share the details with you."

Having considered these four personality types, decide where you "fit in." Having done this, write down where other people that you live with and work with fit in. Have you been communicating with them in the necessary fashion as noted here? What can you do differently tomorrow?

Changing Channels for Better Communication

Once you have considered what personality type you and those around you are, you discover that there are still numerous roadblocks to effective communication. Most people are unaware that all people have preferred communication channels. Have you ever noticed that some people speak very quickly while others communicate very slowly? We all respond to other people's communication in part based upon the tone and pacing of their speech.

THE FAST-PACED COMMUNICATOR

People who speak quickly tend to be visual communicators. These people tend to think and communicate in picture-like descriptions. Slow talkers often perceive "fast talkers" as people who have something to hide and often distrust them. Fast talkers view other fast-talking people as intelligent and "on the ball" people. The moderate talker perceives the fast talker as a bit reckless and quick to jump, but generally in a favorable manner.

People who speak quickly normally use more language that indicates the pictures and movies of their memory that they are describing to you. They also tend to be aware of the boredom factor of other people as listeners, so the "fast talker" often attempts to put too much information into too short a period of time.

THE MODERATELY PACED COMMUNICATOR

People who speak in typical newscaster pacing tend to fall into the category of auditory communicators. They have nice, resonating voices and both prefer to speak and listen to communication at a moderate pace. The auditory communicator will tend to think in words and sounds and enjoy communication with people who are articulate and speak evenly. The slow talker tends to perceive the moderate talker as competent. The fast talker perceives the moderate talker as someone who is a bit less competent than they are. The moderate talker perceives the moderate talker as a kindred spirit, thoughtful, intelligent, and careful.

THE SLOW-PACED COMMUNICATOR

Many people speak at a very slow pace. These people are generally individuals who experience life kinesthetically. They tend to be feeling-oriented people. They may or may not be emotional people, but they are people who rely on their gut instinct and need to see how they feel about something before they respond or enter into communication. The fast talker perceives the slow talker as less intelligent and is often frustrated in communicating with the slow talker. The moderate talker perceives the slow talker in a kind fashion but often is frustrated with the slow response time in communication. The slow talker perceives other slow talkers as kind, good-hearted people who think before sharing their feelings with others. The slow talkers perceive each other as conservative, "look before you jump" types. They view each other as people who are very concerned with the emotional well being of others.

Listening to What They Are Really Saying

The Personality Graph helps us see how people think and communicate differently. There are other behavioral tendencies that are also important to understand before going any further. Each of these tendencies could easily be placed on a graph just like the Thinker/Feeler and Extrovert/Introvert. These tendencies were the first to be discovered and utilized in helping the world understand personality. Now, at the turn of the century, we have identified many new behavioral tendencies that are also known as metaprograms.

The New Metaprograms

There is a definite quality of overlapping programs within each of us. If you watch the NBC news and flip to the CBS news, some of the stories are the same and some are unique to each channel. Metaprograms are similar to this experience. In this section, you will learn some of the "new metaprograms" that are critical to understanding how and why other people communicate as they do. You may feel that there are relationships between two metaprograms. That is a sign that you are becoming consciously aware of the programs that are running through your mind, and a good sign of understanding and utilizing personality traits in communication.

Metaprograms are among the deepest "filters" of perception. These internal sorting patterns unconsciously help us decide what we pay attention to. Metaprograms are, generally speaking, "content free but context dependent." Like a computer software program, one's metaprograms do not actually store information but rather determine what drives one in life. A person's state (of mind) is affected by his metaprograms, which play a significant role in creating internal representations (one's pictures of how he views the world at the conscious and unconscious level).

In order to use a computer program effectively, you must understand how use it. In order to communicate in an efficient manner, you must understand what metaprograms they use. Because metaprograms are deletion and distortion filters that adjust our generalizations (beliefs), we can predict the states of mind of virtually anyone we talk to if we know their metaprograms. If you can predict your client's internal states, you can easily know generally what they are thinking and therefore how best to talk to them.

There are about fifty metaprograms that have been identified as sorting patterns, types, traits, and functions for individuals. You will now learn the "new" metaprograms that most affect the communication process. Remember that all metaprograms exist on a continuum and are not either/or representations of personality! As previously noted, some people are *very* extroverted, and other people may be just a little extroverted. The behavioral distinctions between someone who is extroverted and someone who is *very* extroverted can be described as analogical to a good conversationalist compared to someone who never stops talking to listen.

We have already discussed the four core metaprograms (behavioral tendencies) that Jung, Myers, Briggs, Keirsey, and Bates have so brilliantly educated us about. As you learn about the "new metaprograms," or behavioral tendencies, you will also learn key words and phrases that literally open the doors of the mind you are talking to. How you utilize this powerful information is something you will have to be aware of on your own. The first of the new metaprograms we want to examine is that of the pain/pleasure sorting pattern. This metaprogram is probably the most important metaprogram in talking your way to the top in life.

The Pleasure/Pain Tendency
A. Experience Pleasure..........Avoid Pain

bright future	sick of the way things are
feel great	stop getting hurt
move toward	away from
make new friends	stop being lonely
obtain	get rid of

> *Decades of scientific research clearly show that people are more motivated by pain than by pleasure.*

What this means is that you not only will paint a vivid picture of a wonderful future for your friends and associates when talking to them, but you must also find their current wounds (pain) and heal them. In fact, this one key behavioral tendency drives over a hundred other tendencies and is the foundational key in determining which people will do almost anything to avoid significant pain.

> *People are motivated to move toward pleasure and away from pain. Of the two driving tendencies, most people have been imprinted to move away from pain rather than moving toward pleasure.*

Remember the examples earlier in this book that helped us understand how someone's communication style can be shaped by childhood experiences? Imagine for a moment that you are in sales. Imagine that when one of your customers was a child he was regularly threatened with pain (a spanking, a slap in the face, loss of privileges) when he behaved in a bad way. This developed a powerful behavioral tendency to which many other behavioral tendencies are attached. A smaller number of your customer's parents regularly motivated them as children by offering rewards for good behavior. Most parents use threats of punishment in order to gain compliance. Your customer continues to want to do anything he can to avoid pain. If that means complying with your wishes, that is what he will do.

The Amway Corporation has built one of the largest privately held corporations in the world by pulling the mind strings of those with an entrepreneurial spirit and focusing on the pleasure end of the pain/pleasure metaprogram. They help their distributors build dreams and create vivid and lush futures. They move their distributors toward pleasure, as a rule of thumb.

In contrast, hundreds of the world's largest corporations have built their fortunes by pulling the mind strings of the populace on the pain side of the pain/pleasure metaprogram. History and scientific research have shown that people are very averse to pain. As mentioned above, most people will do far more to avoid pain than experience pleasure. The experience of pain is the driving force of billions of dollars in the advertising industry. How many of these slogans and commercial themes sound familiar to you?

"Aren't you hungry for Burger King, now?"
"Do you suffer from headache pain?"
"Do you feel achy?"
"Can't sleep at night?"

When you are talking with your client or any other listener, your job, in part, is to show how your product or service will create great pleasure if they accept your proposal and also act as a way to avoid pain. If they fail to hire you, you show them how their wound will grow and create pain for them in the future. If they hire you, you will help them heal their wound.

Anthony Robbins, the world's most powerful motivational speaker, got to that pinnacle of success by being able to create vivid pictures of what would happen to people if they didn't allow him to help them. You can utilize the power of the pain/pleasure metaprogram just like Robbins has done.

If you have elicited your listener's metaprograms, then you can focus on the context-specific information you have elicited instead of relying on the general rules we have discussed here. In marketing products, for example, we must rely on the norms. In a direct sales situation, on the other hand, we have a marked advantage of knowing exactly what motivates each specific client.

One effective language pattern that helps the client experience the pain of not working with you is for you to say a variation of the wound opening, "If you don't act on this now, then won't things simply get worse?"

The more the customer fears and moves away from pain, the more likely he is to act now. It is our job to paint a picture of the consequences of failing (for example) to hire you. Experiencing pain must be more than an idea. It must be real to the listener.

If we fail to successfully share our winning ideas that require change, then they are not accepting these ideas because they still associate too much pain to change and we simply have not done our job. Nothing will get a person to change his point of view or buy a product if he is still unconvinced. You must help the person see the obvious and clear benefits, emotional and logical, to accepting your products and services.

Your job as a communicator on the way to the top often is to paint the status quo as miserable. Most people have a fear of change. It is often genetically hard wired within them. When it is not, fear is imprinted early in childhood. Therefore, the status quo must be painted as painful. You must bring out the pain of not changing and make that pain vivid. Someone who finds no drawbacks or very little pain in the status quo will not accept your proposal. They will say no.

The more someone moves away from pain and experiences fear, the more likely he is to act on a decision, now.

The Amway Corporation has utilized a wonderful tool for helping potential distributors feel the pain of failing to become Amway entrepreneurs. For just a moment, pretend you remember when you were first presented with the opportunity to become involved as a distributor. One of the dark pictures the speaker painted for your future was this: If you don't become a distributor, how else are you going to become financially independent? Do you really want to work at that same job forever? Are you really going to be happy with $35,000 per year, every year for the rest of your life?

Does Amway, or *any company or salesperson,* have a right to push these buttons? You bet they do, because they are a company helping make the world go around. Multilevel marketing may or may not be an outstanding entrepreneurial opportunity for any individual, but consider how Amway has become so vast: *Amway utilizes the pain/pleasure metaprogram better than any other private organization in the world.*

THIS EXERCISE IS WORTH $100—DO IT NOW

Use the space below to write down twenty painful futures that your customers or clients could experience if they don't own your product or use your service. Then write down twenty bright futures that your customers or clients will experience if they do use your product or service. The next time you meet with a client you will have a vast array of futures to offer your customer. It is the quality of the images that you help your listener see that will make you thousands of dollars per year in additional business.

Cost/Convenience Tendency

B. Cost.................Convenience

If you are involved in selling or marketing, you should read and understand this tendency carefully. If not, you can move on to the next section. At some point in the sales interview, you will need to determine whether your client is more concerned with speed and convenience or cost.

Many people will take a quick trip to the local convenience store to pick up a few items even though these items cost far more than the grocery store charges. The convenience store is right on the corner and it only takes a minute to get there. It is convenient. The convenience of the store is considered by most to be more important than the increased cost of the goods at the store.

If you are selling financial products, then you'll need to find out whether your client really has the time to closely follow the daily stock reports and make day-to-day decisions about his investments. Would he be happier if you took care of this for him? Is it worth the small cost involved for you to handle his finances in exchange for the burden removed from him?

If you sell real estate, does your buyer really want to commute an extra thirty minutes per day to save $10,000 on the price of a house? You need to find out whether the person is more motivated by cost or convenience before the buying process begins.

Relationship Tendency

C. Match . . . Match/Mismatch . . . Mismatch/Match . . . Polarity

same as	same except	completely different
in common	more	totally changed
like before	progress	one of a kind

Take three coins and place them on the table in front of you. Describe the relationship between those three coins in the space provided.

If you said that the three coins are *all money* or that they are all coins or that they are *all heads* or *all* made of metal, then you are what is known as "a matcher."

If you said that they are all somehow similar but there are also differences, then you would be typed as "a matcher with a mismatch."

If you said something to the effect that "they're all different but they do have this in common," then you are a "mismatcher with a match."

If you found that all three coins were *distinctly different from each other with nothing in common,* then you are what is known as a "polarity responder."

In the real world, you may or may not be able to utilize such a tool. In talking with others, if you needed to instantly know your client's relationship program, you would ask, "What is the relationship between your job (or something similar) this year and last year?" The response you get will be traceable to a point on the continuum. This will help you frame your communication.

Convincer Tendency

D. Internal.....................................External

I think	She thinks
I feel	They tell me
My instincts tell me	Research shows

How does your listener know if he should do something or not? You can ask him how he was convinced the last time he *successfully* made a major decision. You don't want to know how he was convinced of making a big mistake. You want to know how he was convinced of making a good decision.

"Are you glad you bought your current home?"

"Sure, it has been great."

"What convinced you to buy this home?"

Your client will now tell you a story. That story will largely revolve around people and data helping him make his decision or around his gut-level intuition, his feelings. Once you know whether your client is convinced of good decisions by either internal or external sources of information, you can then pace and match that source of information.

"I just had a feeling that it was the right place."

"I want you to tell me if you get that feeling again when we look at the next home we are going to visit."

or

"It matched all of the criteria we set up. It had three bedrooms upstairs, an office, and a swimming pool."

"You mentioned that you are now looking for a larger home with a fireplace and the same nice qualities of your current home. When we come across your next home, let me know right away."

Convincer—# of Times Program

E. Assumed . . . Once . . . Many Times . . . Regularly . . . Always

Some people simply won't listen to you the first time you propose something to them. Some people will need to look at your proprosal numerous times before they decide to take action on it. This being the case, we can elicit their metaprogram for how many times it takes them to see something of quality before they actually decide to take action. Here is another example from the world of sales of determining what a person's behavioral tendency is in the realm of being convinced by something.

"I'm curious. The last time you bought your life insurance, how many times did your agent have to come and show you the benefits of insurance before you actually said okay?"

"We talked about it after the first time he came out. Then he called back and we told him to stop back out the next week. He did and we signed up then."

"Gotcha, so you and Mrs. Johnson appreciate someone who gives you the night to make sure you are doing what is in your best interest, then have me come back out tomorrow. Is that right?"

or

"Well, frankly, we had a pretty hard time deciding whether or not to buy insurance from our guy or not. It was such a great expenditure. I think he was out here three or four times."

"Makes sense to me. I can easily see how difficult it is to make important decisions carefully. What I'd like to do is leave you with several print-outs (proposals). You look them over and I'll stop back tomorrow. Then if you feel you still want to move carefully, I'll stop back next week. Okay?"

Picture Size Tendency

F. General/Big..........................Specific/Detail

Overall	Exactly
The important thing is	Precisely
Generally speaking	To be exact

Do you find that you just *know* when you have done something well, or do you prefer that someone tells you? People who just know they did great have what is called an internal frame of reference. People who prefer to have someone else tell them they did great have an external frame of reference. When you are in communication and you expect someone with an external frame of reference to know whether she did a good job and you don't want to tell her, you do her a great disservice. On the other hand, if you tell her that she did great you open the lines of communication because she needs the external validation. Similarly, offering your validation too often to someone with a strong internal frame of reference will not be accepted in a positive light. People with a strong internal frame of reference normally do not want a lot of validation or external feedback of any kind.

People with a strong internal frame of reference will be more at ease with you when you use phrases like "What do you think," "How do you feel," "What do your instincts tell you," and so on. You want to set these people at ease by finding out how they feel inside. On the other hand, people with a strong external frame of reference will feel more comfortable when you tell them they did well. They will feel more comfortable when they hear "She told me that you . . ." "They tell me that you . . ." "Research shows that you made a good decision . . ."

Another way of looking at this tendency is in the active persuasion process.

Have you ever noticed that many people you talk to get bored to tears when you start going over the details and nuances of your ideas, products, and services? These people are what we call "big picture" people. On the other hand, other people will feel that you are trying to cheat them if you just give them a few broad strokes of information. They want all the details. Anything short of a full disclaimer and a detailed future amortization puts you in their dog house, and they won't listen to you. These people are "detail listeners."

People who are rushed for time generally need you to put your proposal into a four-minute communication. If they want more information, they will ask for it as you then become a priority in their day. This may or may not mean that you literally talk faster. It does mean that regardless of what you are talking about, you should be able to discuss your idea intelligently for twenty seconds, twenty minutes or two hours. You will meet people who will buy a car in twenty seconds and a house in twenty minutes. You will also meet people who won't buy anything until they have had hours, days, weeks, or months to consider it. Be aware of their Picture-Size Program, and you will enhance the probabilty of your being on the same wavelength as your listener.

How do you find out someone's tendency as far as whether they are a general listener or a specific listener? Ask something like: "When you bought your last car, how long did you actually have to think about it before you told the salesman yes? Did he give you all the specs on the vehicle or did you just see it and say, 'Hey, that's a nice car. I'll take it.'"

People who have a big-picture size tendency normally are made to feel at ease by phrases like "Overall," "The important thing is," and "Generally speaking." People who like to hear a lot of details will feel comfortable with you when they hear words like "Exactly," "Precisely," and "To be exact."

Possibility/Necessity Tendency

G. Possibility.............................Necessity

Opportunity	Must
Chance	If need be
Could happen	Only if

Here is an example from the world of selling again. Does your client buy your financial products because he *needs* a nest egg at retirement or because it expands the *possibilities* of how he can live his retirement years? The distinction can be very important.

You must propose your ideas, products, and services through the same filters as your clients' metaprograms for instant compliance. If your client invests in mutual funds because it will afford him the *opportunity* to travel abroad and have freedom, then he is a possibility investment buyer. Another salesperson attempting to sell to him because he'll need the money to replace Social Security will fail to make the sale because he has not utilized the filter.

A useful question to find out whether the person tends to be possibility or necessity thinking is,

"Why are you in the business you are in?"

Your client either had to get the job he has or start the business he owns, or else he saw this job or business as an opportunity or possibility for some brighter future. Once you know which end of the spectrum your client is on, you operate through that filter as well. As with all metaprograms, if you pace the client's metaprogram and work within those filters, you will gain rapid compliance.

What are the similarities and the differences between the Possibility/Necessity metaprogram and the Pleasure/Pain metaprogram? What differences do you notice?

Change/Status Quo Tendency

H. Change...............................Status Quo

Different	Consistent
Evolve	Stable
Alter	Steady
Switch	Same

Does your client like things to stay the way they are? Does he like to see his business or himself evolve? Grow? Does he like to change? Does he need to keep the status quo?

If you know the buyer's Change/Status Metaprogram, you have a grand opportunity to create security in the status quo or excitement in change.

People who like change rarely keep jobs for a long period of time. They tend to get bored easily, and they are constantly trying new things. People who like the status quo will tend to stay in the same jobs and do the same things day after day, month after month, year after year.

Accept Readily/Skeptical-Closed Program

I. Accepting.........Cautious.........Skeptical..........Closed

understand	careful beware	never
unconditional	consider	can't
always	sometimes	makes no sense
friendly	nervous	afraid not

You will discover that your listeners fall on a continuum from open acceptance to critical skepticism of new ideas. This tendency has some similarities to that of Change/Status Quo. However, they are not the same. People who are accepting are willing to listen. Those who are closed are usually closed because of some event(s) that have transpired in their lives. Interestingly, people who are closed to opinions often got that way because they were once vulnerable and got hurt or taken advantage of. These are the people who put up "No Soliciting" signs. As every sales-person knows, they are among the easiest people to gain compliance with.

Perception Tendency

How do you perceive the world? This depends on whether you are an Intuiting or a Sensing personality type. The Intuitive person is directed by the unconscious mind to a far greater degree than the person who is a Sensor. The Sensor is guided by five senses and specific verifiable experiences. Sensors tend to not worry about the past or the future. They are here one day at a time. Sensors tend to pay close attention to facts and information. They are very aware of what their five senses are experiencing moment by moment. Sensors tend to be very good at mastering a set of skills once they have learned them.

The Intuitive person may often seem unaware of all that is going on around him. He feels comfortable listening to stories and may talk in metaphors a great deal. Intuitive people love imagery and will listen to you more keenly when you have a story to tell them. Intuitive people tend to attempt to understand the connections and interconnections between people, the deeper aspects of spirituality, and so on. They are not content to simply take the facts as the facts. Intuitive people tend to get bored once they have learned something new. Therefore they go on to new horizons much more rapidly than the Sensing personality.

People who tend to be guided by their intuition are most at ease when they hear words like hunch, future, speculate, inspiration, fantasy, possible, fiction, ingenious, and imaginative. People who are of the Sensing personality type are more at ease when they hear words that are verifiable in a context. These might include words like perspiration, past, realistic, actual, down to earth, no-nonsense, fact, practical, and sensible.

About two-thirds of all English-speaking people are Sensing personality types.

Closure Tendency

The final behavioral tendency is closure. There are two extremes on this continuum. One is the Judging personality type and the other is the Perceiving personality type. The Judging personality is someone who deals with the outer world in a more or less black-and-white fashion. The Perceiver sees the outer world and accepts it, more or less, for what it is. When judging begins, perception ends. The two attitudes do not normally occur simultaneously, as in other tendencies.

A person will accept communication or discussion until enough information has transpired, and then a judgment is made. Similarly, a person will suspend judgment until he has enough perceived information. The distinction with this continuum is what the person is comfortable with. Do people prefer to come to judgment or do they prefer to consider and perceive? Judging personalities tend to put order in their lives. Perceivers simply tend to live their lives and go with the flow.

The Judging personality type is one that really likes to plan the events of the day, the week, and the year. The Perceiver, on the other hand, is more likely to want to live for the moment and go with the flow. They like to be spontaneous.

Judging people tend to make quick decisions, while the Perceiver usually experiences stress in the decision-making process. The Judging person likes closure, and the sooner the better. Because the Judging person makes quick decisions and feels good about it, they tend to be authoritative in their communication appearance. The Perceivers like to keep their options open and therefore appear to vacillate in the decision-making process. They do not appear to be in control because they are slower to judgment.

People who are of the Judging personality type tend to be right on time, if not a few minutes early. Similarly the Judging personality is one that tends to get all of the work done before engaging in pleasure activities. They are good at delaying gratification. The Perceiver of course wonders why people would ever stress out over a few minutes of time. Perceivers tend to be late and don't feel bad about it, not one bit. In the same vein, the Perceiving personality tends to be a procrastinator.

People with Judging personality types tend to feel comfortable when they hear words like settled, decided, fixed, plan ahead, run one's life, closure, decision-making, planned, and completed. Perceiving personality types tend to feel more at ease when they hear words and phrases that include the ideas of pending, gather more data, flexible, adapt as you go, let life happen, keep your options open, "treasure hunting," open-ended, and emergent.

The English-speaking population is split about fifty-fifty in this behavioral tendency.

In the next chapter you will move from the mind to the face and the body. What is your body saying anyway? Is it helping your climb to the top, or is it holding you back? Turn the page and find out what very few people know!

CHAPTER 7

Can You Hear Your Body Talking?

Y OUR BODY LANGUAGE AND PHYSICAL APPEARANCE will boost you to the top or keep you among the majority of people in the middle and bottom. You have less than ten seconds and, realistically, closer to four seconds to make a good first impression on those you come into contact with. There is a world of research that clearly indicates that you will be judged professionally and personally in the first few seconds of your meeting someone for the first time. In fact, your first impression is recorded and is used as a yardstick for all future communication by those you meet. Whatever that first impression is going to be on your part, you want it to be intentional and with a purpose.

Before going any further, we need to take a look at how to talk your way to the top with your body. Most people are completely unaware of just how much their body says and how it often contradicts what the words are saying! There are numerous elements of what we might call body language. They include your physical features, both changeable and unchangeable, your gestures and signals that you send to others at the conscious and unconscious level, and the space that you use when communicating with others. In this chapter we will touch on all of these important areas of body language.

What You Look Like Really Talks

Let's begin with our physical appearance. Here are some astounding facts that will give you pause for thought when you consider how important appearance is in getting to the top.

Your perceived level of attractiveness by other people will be a significant benefit or detriment in your life. It isn't fair, but it is true. People who get to the top learn how to deal with less than perfect physical features and work with what they have. Before we consider just how to increase your face value, look at the results of some fascinating studies about physical appearance.

The Power of Physical Appearance

Did you know that in university settings, professors who are considered physically attractive by students are regarded as better teachers on the whole than unattractive professors? Attractive professors are also more likely to be asked for help on problems. These same attractive professors also tend to receive positive recommendations from other students to take their classes and also are less likely to receive the blame when a student receives a failing grade! (Romano and Bordieri, 1989)

Did you know that marriage and dating decisions are often made with great weight placed on physical attractiveness? A wide variety of research indicates that men will often reject women who are lacking (in their opinion) in positive physical features. Women on the other hand place less significance in a man's physical attractiveness in considering him for a date or marriage. (Studies by R. E. Baber)

Did you know that in studies done on college campuses, it has been proven that attractive females (attraction as perceived by the professors) receive significantly higher grades than male students or relatively unattractive females? (Studies by J. E. Singer)

There is more evidence that shows you must make the most of what you have physically.

Among strangers, individuals perceived as unattractive in physical appearance are generally undesirable for any interpersonal relationship! (Studies by D. Byrne, O. London, K. Reeves)

In one significant study of fifty-eight unacquainted men and women in a social setting, after a first date, 89 percent of the people who wanted a second date decided that because of the attractiveness of the partner! (Brislin and Lewis)

In the persuasion process, attractive females are far more convincing than females perceived as unattractive. (Mills and Aronson)

Among American women, the size of a woman's bust is significant to how both American men and women perceive the woman. Women with a "medium-sized" bust are considered to be more likable and have greater personal appeal than women with a large or a small bust. Women with a small bust are perceived as more intelligent, competent, and moral. Women with a large bust are generally perceived as less intelligent and less competent. (Kleinke, Staneski, 1980)

In yet another study, we find that young men who are obese are generally considered to be slothful and lazy. Both men and women who are obese are generally perceived to have personality characteristics that place them at a disadvantage in social and business settings. (Worsley, 1981)

Can You Change Your Appearance?

Study after study reveals that how you look is critical to someone's first impression of you. So what can you do to change how you look? You can't change everything about your physical appearance, but you can definitely make changes that will give you a booster shot at going to the top in your business and your personal life.

Research studies tell us that the "exposure principle" increases our "face value." Specifically, the exposure principle says that the more often you are seen by someone the more attractive and intelligent you appear to them. If you weren't gifted with a Cindy Crawford or Tom Cruise face then it's time for you to take advantage of the exposure principle.

If you don't have the advantage of being "seen" time after time by a person or a group, then you must make the most of what you have. In other words, you want to look as good as you possibly can on every given day. Because of the significance of body image and weight, you must do what you can to keep your body weight down and your body in shape. It will help make your overall image to be as good as it can be.

Your teeth will tell a tale as well. If your teeth are yellow and look like you just ate, your face value is obviously greatly reduced. Do everything you can to keep your teeth pearly white and you will be perceived as more attractive. (You've already seen the benefits of the perception of attractiveness.) When you watch the news tonight on television, look at the teeth of every news anchor, weather person, and sports announcer. They all have beautiful white teeth. There's a reason for that, and that is positive impression management. You do the same and you will have a boost on the way to the top.

Hair is significant to how you assess other people, isn't it? Hairstyles can say a great deal about a person. Women with short and stylish hair tend to be perceived as more professional. Older women with longer hair tend to be perceived as women who really wish they were much younger. Men who are balding and try any of several ways to "cover up" look as though they suffer from self-esteem challenges. Men who have long hair tend to be indifferent toward what others think of them. Men whose hair is trimmed, styled, and short tend to be perceived as professional. What is your hairstyle saying about you?

You've now heard some of the important facts about enhancing your personal appearance. Now, let's look at how you can do even more to enhance your face value.

20 Tips to Look Great for Your Climb to the Top

Both female and male sales professionals make mistakes that can cost thousands of dollars in income every year. It is interesting that our research indicates that women will far outsell men of the same skill and knowledge level *if their appearance is perceptually correct.* Women in selling make far more mistakes with their appearance than men do.

In our everyday life, women tend to choose their spouses based on two factors: resources (money, education, or potential income) and physical attractiveness. Women rank resources as the most desirable characteristic in a spouse and physical attractiveness as second. For men, it is the opposite. Men are very interested in physical attractiveness and normally find resources far less significant.

Remember, study after study shows that physical attractiveness is very important in one person's perception of another person. Eighty-nine percent of all people on their first date decided "yes" or "no" to a second date on the basis of the physical attractiveness of the other person!

Remember the studies that show that men will reject women on the basis of what they perceive as deficiencies in the woman's appearance. (In the realm of interpersonal relations, women are more interested in resources than men, showing some practicality but continuing the thread of superficiality in this area!)

Many elements of your physical appearance are genetic and are not going to change. You can't grow two more inches and you can't change the shape of your face. There is much you can do, however, to enhance your perceived physical attractiveness. Here are the keys to appearance for both men and women. Follow these twenty tips, and you will increase your face value as you glide to the top:

1) Women: Never dress suggestively in business. Research shows that you will get a longer interview, but you will make fewer sales and change fewer minds in business meetings. Dressing suggestively pulls out an entirely different set of mental perceptions than you want! Low-cut blouses and shirts are out at work. Mini-skirts are out in the business arena as well. In social settings they can speak volumes, but what they communicate in business is a lack of seriousness and professionalism.

2) Women: Believe it or not, if your wedding ring is large and you are going to be seeing women in a sales situation, take it off and put your band on instead. A large wedding ring reduces sales. Women outwardly express their excitement about a large wedding ring, but it is perceived as a negative for numerous reasons. Your sales will go down if your wedding ring is significantly larger than that of your customer.

3) Women: If your fingernails are more than half an inch long, cut them and you will increase your perceived intelligence by those with whom you communicate. Long fingernails are perceived negatively by men and women in the world of business.

4) Men and Women: If your fingernails look like anything but clean and well rounded, get a manicure. Your fingers are one area that can turn off both men and women. A professional communicator on his way to the top has nice looking hands.

5) Men and Women: If you wear glasses, smaller glasses are usually appropriate. You are usually better off making presentations wearing contact lenses, if they do not irritate your eyes too much. Glasses rarely make sales and can often break them.

6) Men and Women: Your weight will make or break your verbal message in many different communications. If you are more than 20 percent over the normal weight for your height, you lose credibility in both the corporate and personal world. Begin a program of eating right and activity to reduce your waistline. Thinner people are perceived as more intelligent and more attractive. Period.

7) Men: Facial hair reduces sales and generally is a weakness in other settings. If you have a beard, you might want to cut it now (unless it is covering a scar of some kind). There are no men with beards in the top 100 sales professionals and few bearded men at the top of the public speaking profession or corporate America. If you have a mustache, ask men and women for their opinion. Some men appear to look better with a mustache, but, in general, facial hair reduces credibility.

8) Men and Women: Ear and nose hair can create feelings of disgust in many of your dates, clients, and customers. If you look in the mirror and you see ear or nose hair, cut it and keep it cut.

9) Women: Makeup that is lightly applied is not distracting. If your makeup is heavy, you will lose credibility. The closer to "natural" you appear, the better.

10) Men and Women: Teeth. Teeth should be white, flossed, and clean before you meet any customer. If you teeth are stained, get them cleaned. Yellowed teeth lose sales.

11) Men: Hair Length. If your hair length goes beyond covering the back of your neck, you will lose credibility. Long hair can feel good and even look good, but it isn't taken seriously. Decide whether you want to make a predictably great first impression or whether you want your hair long.

12) Men and Women: Dress like your customers and clients dress . . . plus 10 percent. If you see conservative clients, dress very conservatively. If you are spending time with casual clients, you should dress "dressy casual."

13) Men and Women: When wearing suit coats, nothing goes in the outer pocket except a spotless and perfectly fitted handkerchief. Contrary to popular belief among some men, the outer pocket on your jacket is not a storage area for pens, rulers, and calculators. Nothing else goes in the suit coat outer pocket except that handkerchief.

14) Men and Women: Your shoes should be shiny and looking new. The rule of thumb is that you should never wear shoes that aren't shined, and if you don't like to wear shoes that you have to shine, choose a style that doesn't require constant upkeep on your part.

15) Men and Women: Jewelry. Men should wear nothing other than a watch and a wedding band. Women should wear nothing more than a watch, a wedding ring or band, a thin necklace, and a pin. A small pair of women's earrings are acceptable, but they should not distract. Earrings for men are always out. In the world of business, no earrings are permissible for men if you are to be perceived as credible by the majority of the people on the way to the top.

16) Men and Women: You should be showered every morning and have your hair conservatively and neatly in place before every meeting or personal get together.

17) Men: Your briefcase should be no larger than a case that will hold two copies of *Encyclopedia Britannica.* What does it say if you walk into a meeting with a brief case that looks like a piece of luggage? Disorganized.

18) Women: A large purse is out. Never bring a large purse into meetings where your credibility is important. If you do, you will look disorganized. Bring a trim purse with whatever essentials you need during the day. Everything else can stay in the car or in your desk at the office.

19) Men: Your suit should fit properly. With your coat buttoned, take your fist and place it between your belly button and the coat. It should comfortably touch both. If you can't squeeze your fist comfortably between your stomach and your coat, your coat is too small. In important business meetings, you should be aware that most people can tell the difference between a $100 suit and a $400 suit, even if you can't. When it is time to look your best, do so.

20) Men: Your pants should touch the "bridge" on your shoes. They should not run on the ground or be raised high on your socks. If they don't touch your shoes, get them altered. Anything unusual costs you sales, and that means you lose credibility.

Saying Hello and Shaking Hands: Merging the Verbal and Non-Verbal

What should be the most natural thing in the world has become one of the most difficult. How do you say hello to your client?

Walk into the office with excellent posture, taking medium-length strides, and say, "Hi, I'm Kevin Hogan, the author of *The Psychology of Persuasion.* You're John, right? Nice to meet you."

On the word John, you shake hands. If you walk into the office and your customer takes the lead by introducing himself, simply follow his lead and shake hands as he extends his.

Hold his hands for two or three beats and gently release it. Assuming you shake hands with your right hand, your left hand should *not* take part in this ritual. Here are the ten keys to shaking hands properly.

TEN DOS AND DON'TS OF SHAKING HANDS

- Always maintain eye contact when shaking hands.
- Do not use the infamous two-hand handshake.
- Do not grab your client's elbow with your left hand.
- Do not hold your client's hand for more than two seconds.

• Do not crush your client's hand.
• Do not try to get a better grip than your customer.
• Do not have a limp handshake.
• Your hand should be firm but under control.
• Your hands should be dry and warm.
• Keep your left arm and hand out of the greeting.

Where You Sit Can Change How People Look at You!

Standing in someone's office is a problem that will need an immediate solution. As soon as pleasantries are exchanged, you and your customer should be seated. If you are both standing for an extended period of time and your customer doesn't have the forethought to offer you a chair, then you can ask, "Should we sit down and be comfortable?" Unless you are in a retail environment, sales are not made and deals are not negotiated standing up.

You may have an option of considering where to sit. If so, you are in luck. Scientific research is on your side in telling you exactly where to sit. Seating options normally occur on lunch or dinner dates at a restaurant and in meeting rooms. If you are in a restaurant, quickly search out (with your eyes) a location that allows you to sit facing the majority of the people in the restaurant so your client is obligated to sit facing you, away from the clientele and staff of the restaurant. Booth seating is ideal.

Your partner's or client's attention should be on you, not the waitress, bus boy, and the dozens of other people in the restaurant. Your seat selection will assure you his attention. Once you have the attention of your customer, only you can make your presentation or engage in conversation.

How Do You Select Seating?

Ideally, you can create a seating arrangement that is most likely to facilitate the communication process. Here are the key rules in seating selection:

1) As a rule, if you have already met your client or friend and you know he is right-handed, for example, attempt to sit to his right. If he is left-handed, sit to his left.

2) If you are a woman attempting to communicate effectively with

another woman, sitting opposite of each other is as good or better than sitting at a right angle.

3) If you are a woman attempting to persuade a man to your way of thinking, the best option is to be at a right angle if at all possible.

4) If you are a man attempting to persuade a man, you should be seated across from each other in the booth setting if possible.

5) If you are a man attempting to communicate well with a female in business or in a social setting, you should be seated across from her at a smaller, more intimate table.

What Do You Do After You Are Seated?

Waiting for the waitress to come in a restaurant can be awkward if you do not know your date or your client very well. If you are meeting your client in his office, you will immediately get down to business after brief pleasantries. (It should be noted that sometimes pleasantries do NOT have to be brief. Many of my biggest and best presentations were made in the last two minutes of meetings that would extend to two hours discussing everything from baseball to sex to religion. The level of rapport and quality of mutual interests will ultimately be your guide.)

Once seated, keep your hands away from your face and hair. There is nothing good that your fingers can do above your neck while you are meeting with a client. The best salespeople in the world have wonderful control of their gestures. They know, for example, that when their hands are further from their body than their elbows they are going to be perceived in a more flamboyant manner.

While you are seated, if you are unfamiliar with your date or client, it is best that you keep both feet on the floor. This helps you maintain control and good body posture. People who are constantly crossing and uncrossing their feet and legs are perceived as less credible. And people who keep one foot on their other knee when talking have a tendency to shake the free foot, creating a silly-looking distraction. Feet belong on the floor.

Meanwhile, your hands will say a great deal about your comfort level. If you are picking at the fingers of one hand, you are pushing buttons in your listener that reveal fear or discomfort. This is picked up by the unconscious mind of the customer and makes him feel uncomfortable. If you don't know what to do with your hands and you are female, cup your right hand face down into your left hand, which is face up. Don't squeeze your hands. Simply let them lie together on your lap.

For men, the best thing to do is to keep your hands separate unless you begin to fidget, at which point you will follow the advice for your female counterpart noted above.

How Close Is TOO Close?

Whether seated or standing, you should stay out of your client's "intimate space." Intimate space is normally defined as an eighteen-inch bubble around the entire body of your client. Entering this space is done so at your own risk. This doesn't mean that you can't share a secret with your date or your client. This doesn't mean you can't touch your date or your client. It does mean that if you enter into "intimate space," you are doing so strategically and with a specific intention. There can be great rewards when entering intimate space, but there are also great risks, so be thoughtful about your client's "space." Similarly, if you leave the "casual-personal" space of a client, which is nineteen feet, four inches, you also are at risk of losing the focus of attention of the client. Ideally, most of your communication with a new customer should be at a distance of two to four feet, measuring nose to nose. This is appropriate. Generally, you begin communication at the four-foot perimeter and slowly move closer as you build rapport with your client.

What Is Effective Eye Contact?

Eye contact is critical in any face-to-face meeting. As a rule of thumb, you should maintain eye contact with your client two-thirds of the time and with a date about 80 percent of the time. This doesn't mean that you look at her eyes for twenty minutes then away for ten minutes. It does mean that you keep in touch for about seven seconds then away for about three seconds, or in touch for about fourteen seconds and away for about six seconds. Eye contact doesn't mean just gazing into the eyes. Eye contact is considered any contact in the "eye-nose" triangle. If you create a triangle from the eyes to the nose of the customer, you have the "eye-nose" triangle. This is the area where you want to focus 65-70 percent of eye contact.

Should you sense that your client is uncomfortable at this level, reduce your eye contact time. Many people who were born and reared in the

Orient (Japan, for example) are not accustomed to the degree of eye contact that Americans are.

Eyes are a fascinating part of the human body. When a person finds someone or something very appealing to him, his pupil size (the black part of the eyes) grows significantly larger. This is one of the few parts of body language that is absolutely uncontrollable by the conscious mind. You simply cannot control your pupil size. If you are interested in someone else, your pupil size will grow dramatically. If someone else is interested in you, their pupils will grow larger when looking at you, and there is nothing they can do about it. This is one of the powerful predictors of liking in non-verbal communication.

It should be noted that pupils will also get larger in situations of extreme fear and when a setting is dark. Pupils expand to let more light in like a camera. When the setting is very well lit, the pupils will contract to the size of a very tiny little dot.

If you follow the tips in this chapter for improving your appearance, being careful about appropriate dress, and are careful with your use of space, you will be on your way to the top in personal relationships and in business.

There are two other telling behaviors relating to the eyes.

First, if someone is blinking far more rapidly than they normally do, that is usually an indicator of annoying lighting in the setting you are in or of anxiety and/or lying on the part of the person. In 1998 President Clinton gave a short speech offering his reasons for having an illicit affair with Monica Lewinsky. During this speech his eyes blinked a momentous 120 times per minute. Two days later he gave a speech about a U.S. bombing raid on a terrorist group overseas. In this speech his eye blinks were about thirty-five per minute. The difference is extremely important in evaluating the comfort level and honesty of the president in each situation. If someone is blinking far more often than normal (and you do have to know what is normal for each person you meet, and adjust for lighting), you know they are very probably extremely anxious and very possibly lying.

Second, if you are in conversation with someone and their eyes are easily distracted by the goings on in the environment, this is usually a good indicator that you haven't earned the interest of your listener. In general, it is a very wise strategy for you to keep your eyes trained on your date or business associate in distracting environments. To constantly look around at the environment when you are with someone else is perceived as rude.

To keep eye contact with another person instead of being distracted by extraneous activity is considered flattering and complimentary, especially by women.

Let Your Body Do the Talking in Group Presentations

Everything you have read up until this point applies to group presentations. Presentations before larger numbers of people simply offer a few more challenges and a few greater rewards. If you are presenting to a group, you already know that you have something important enough to say to get the attention of the group. No one in the group showed up by accident.

Know what you are going to say in advance. You don't have to write out your presentation. In fact, unless you are the president of the United States, no one will listen if you do. There are a few keys to speaking before groups. One is seat selection. If you are the key speaker and will be speaking from the one and only table, you want to sit on an end or in the middle of one of the two sides.

If you have any known detractors of your idea, product, or service, you should have them sit to your immediate left or immediate right. These are the least powerful positions on the table. Notice that in presidential press conferences where members of both parties are seated at a table, President Clinton always has the house Republican leaders seated immediately next to him. These positions have no focal attention, and people sitting here rarely speak with any credibility.

If you have to speak before a group and use a podium, you have an opportunity to make or break a sale by a strategy that I discovered by watching television evangelists. This strategy takes some time to master, but is remarkably effective.

Strategic Movement

The most powerful non-verbal process you can use with an audience that must determine as a group to "buy" or "not buy" your ideas, products, or services is that of strategic movement. Other sales trainers call similar strategies spatial anchoring. Both are applicable, and here is what strategic movement is all about.

Do you remember Johnny Carson? He was the host of "The Tonight Show" for almost thirty years, before Jay Leno took over in the 1990s.

Each night when Johnny came out he stood on a small star that marked exactly where he was supposed to stand. It was the best spot on the entire stage for camera angles and for connecting with the audience. Because of the curtain backdrop, we knew without seeing Johnny's face that it was he and not a guest host, who would stand on a different star.

The only thing Johnny ever did from this specific location was make people laugh. He didn't wander around the stage and tell his jokes. He stood right there and made people laugh. There were many nights when Johnny literally could just stand on his star and people would laugh. That is spatial anchoring. Audience laughter was anchored (conditioned to) Johnny's standing on his star.

When I first visited NBC in 1984, I thought it was fascinating that only Johnny stood on that star. At the time, I thought it was an ego trip or some bit of arrogance on the part of Carson. How wrong I was. I knew nothing at that time of spatial anchoring and strategic movement.

When you are called on to make your sales presentation (or any kind of a proposal) in front of a group, you are on stage. You are the star. You will want to select three specific points on the stage, or in the meeting room, from which to speak. Each of these points is a specific location and not an approximate area. Point "A" is your podium. Podiums and lecterns are used by teachers and preachers. Normally these unconscious links are not positive reminders of younger days. Therefore, *the podium (point "A") will always be used only to relay factual information to your audience.*

You will choose a point to your left about four feet from your podium from which you will deliver all of the bad news discussed in your presentation. (You can't make many sales without painting a vivid picture about how bad things will get if the corporation doesn't hire you.) The bad news spot is point "B," and you will only talk there about problems and things that will be perceived as "bad" by your audience.

Point "C" will be approximately two and one-half feet to the right of the podium, and you will always paint uplifting, positive, exciting, motivating pictures from this location. Everything we want the audience to agree with will be discussed from this point after we establish this as the "good news point."

Imagine that you are giving your presentation to this group and you need to be very persuasive. My favorite example here is that of fund raising for a charity. Your job? Get a big check for your favorite charity.

You place your folder or notes on the podium and immediately walk to "B" point. You tell a story about a hurting child or a suffering individual. You then explain how this one incident is far from isolated. You move to the podium. You expound the facts and figures about the gravity of the problem that you are asking the group to help solve by making a big donation.

Now you move to point "C," where you will become excited about how the charitable organization is currently solving the problems and helping the suffering you talked about at "B." Everything that is good and wonderful you will "anchor" into point "C."

As you conclude your speech, you will have a path that you have laid. You have moved from A to B to C to B to A several times. *You conclude on point "C" because it is the good news point and offers each person an opportunity to participate in healing the wounds you opened at "B."*

The truly unique tactic in strategic movement is the ability to subtly answer questions at the unconscious level without saying anything significant on the conscious level. Imagine that the audience is given the opportunity for questions and answers with you. An individual in the audience asks you about the possibility of donating to a competing charitable organization.

"Well, of course, you know that is a good charity, and there would be nothing wrong with that . . . of course . . . (walking to point "C") by taking advantage of the plan that we have, we can accomplish all of the goals that you have for the community. I'm sure you realize it is up to you to make it happen. We can only help those who need it if you make a decision tonight."

Discussing the other charity in a neutral or slightly positive manner from point "B" allows you to unconsciously associate all of the negative feelings to your "competitor," and you solve the problem as you move to the "C" point. *If you find this manipulative, then you are working for the wrong charity. If anyone else is more qualified to help a group, sells a better product, or offers a better service, you should be working for them!*

There is no more powerful manner of utilizing space than spatial anchoring combined with strategic movement. The next time you watch a great speaker, notice how he or she utilizes strategic movement. If the speaker stays at the podium, notice how all the good news is given while gesturing with hand "A," and all the bad news is discussed when gesturing with the other hand. The greatest speakers are masters of spatial anchoring and strategic movement. As you develop skill in spatial anchoring and strategic movement, you can literally push buttons in people for various states of mind, including anger, love, happiness, and peace of mind simply by moving from point to point.

CHAPTER 8

Talking Your Way
to the Top in the Workplace

IF YOU ARE GOING TO THE TOP in the workplace, there are two major requirements.

1) You must know what is important to the people at the top in the workplace.

2) You must be able to *artfully* communicate to people that you have what it takes to be at the top.

Virtually every major corporation resembles a pyramid when the power and income levels are charted on paper. Structurally speaking, a pyramid has a lot of people at the "bottom," a smaller but significant number in the middle, and a few at the "top."

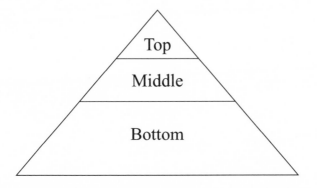

Question: How do you get from the 80 percent of the people living at the base of the corporation through the 15 percent in the middle to the 5 percent on top? We know that in major corporations over 75 percent of all significant moves up the corporate ladder are facilitated by a mentor. In other words, a person at the bottom forged a relationship with someone at or near the top. Then the person near the top coached and helped the person in the base of the pyramid move to the next level. In order for you to participate in this channel to the top, you must be able to communicate with people at the top. If you don't build relationships with people that are further up the ladder, you will in all likelihood work in the base of the pyramid ad infinitum.

There is a saying in the business world that goes like this: "It's not what you know but who you know." That is only partially true. You can know the president of the company himself, but if you aren't competent in the skill areas he values most you still won't survive at the top.

Do you know the secrets of success in the corporate area? You might guess that they involve technical skill or specific corporate knowledge. You would have to guess again! If executives could pick just one key skill they wanted to see in their employees, what would that skill be? In 1998, the skills, talents, and abilities that executives looked for most in their employees were assessed and reported in *Investors Business Daily* (December 18, 1998):

Integrity and Honesty	16%
People Skills	12%
Action Oriented	11%
Creativity	10%
Goal Orientation	8%
Attention to Detail	7%
Persistence	7%
Positive Thinking	7%
Vision	6%
Dollar Management	6%
Ongoing Learning	5%
Time Management	5%

It should be noted that although executives clearly favor people with good people skills (communication, listening, high degree of ethics), most executives do NOT perceive themselves as being at the top of the ladder when it comes to dealing with other people. They clearly admire these skills in other people. They clearly want to see people who have these skills get to the top. Why? People who can communicate effectively are difficult to replace. Anyone can answer a phone. Not everyone can defuse the irate customer on the other end. Everyone in the company knows about the company products, but very few currently possess the skills necessary to sell other people on their company's products.

Clearly, if you want to get to the top of your business, you will have to talk your way there. Effective communication will make the difference between success and failure in business for most people. *Somehow those around you must begin to see the qualities listed above emanating from you.* Here are a few key ideas on how to make sure that your best feet are getting put forward. You can't go around telling people that you possess all of these qualities. People must perceive that you have these traits from the conversations you have with others.

Integrity and Honesty

Have you ever heard anyone say that they had integrity or that they were honest? After you heard that, did you realize that you doubted the person? Why? Because the words integrity and honesty are so powerful that they immediately bring to mind their opposite characteristics! Therefore, people must not hear you say that you are "an honest person" or that you "work for an honest company." No one wants to hear about "the integrity of your company." *Don't talk about the honesty or integrity of anyone or anything you want people to perceive as honest or having integrity.*

So how do you let people know that you are honest person who holds integrity in high regard? You must communicate about others in a fashion that makes it obvious that you have integrity and are honest. "Why didn't the president just come out and say he 'did it?' That would have been the honest thing to do." The comment is about another person's conduct and indicates that you hold no malice toward the person, only that you wish he had communicated honestly. "I hope that someday doing the right thing comes back into vogue."

Comment on the wonderful things that people do that show their integrity and honesty. When you hear about someone returning a lost wallet or purse and you're in the lunchroom at work, let others know that you are impressed with that action. Then wonder aloud whether or not you should have been really that impressed. After all, isn't that what you would expect?

People Skills

What are people skills? People skills are the ability to communicate effectively with other people. People skills include dealing with difficult customers, fellow employees who are a pain to cope with, and representing your division, office, or company in grand fashion in person and on the phone.

People skills take some time to develop. Sometimes the Socializer personality is a natural at people skills though they do tend to go on and on, on occasion! *People skills are best defined as the skills necessary to build and maintain rapport with other people.*

In the preceding chapter we talked about building rapport through matching communication styles. The information that you learned there will help you in all of your corporate dealings.

If you want to go to the top in your office, division, or company, there is really nothing more important than being effective in dealing with and handling people in business.

Action Oriented

How do people know you are an "action-oriented person?" Like all of the other traits, you can't brag about this. Once again you must let people hear you communicate your orientation to action in your daily communication:

"You know, it always fascinates me that people will wait until the last minute before beginning a project that they know will be critical to the office. Then, of course, they don't finish on time and other projects add up on the way. Do you know what I mean?"

This says that you have already had the forethought to think through and participate in action-oriented thinking. Another example:

"I remember one time a bunch of us were given twenty leads each to call at the office. I really wanted them all because I was one person who really got on the phone and in front of the clients as soon as possible. I always figured that procrastination was practicing for death."

Creativity

Creativity is important in developing products, problem solving, and taking old ideas and putting a new spin on them to improve what once was without changing everything overnight.

It's usually best that people see your creativity in small and financially efficient ways before recommending moving your company headquarters, changing anything too dramatically, or even altering clothing styles too much. However, when you begin to make small changes that work within the company, you will begin to be seen as a visionary.

When communicating with others about creativity, note what another company did that worked in a similar situation and comment about the creative genius behind the idea. This allows others to see that you are indeed creative and that you might just be the person to go to when something similar comes up in your office.

Goal Orientation

What you don't say might speak volumes when it comes to goals and strategic thinking. How can someone know you are a goal-oriented person without your talking about your own goals and your own goal-achievement history? Consider asking questions that reflect in-depth thinking:

"What is the company's goal for growth this year?"

"What is our sales objective for the month?"

"What does corporate want to see us net this quarter?"

"What would it take for our stock price to go up 10 percent?"

All of these questions show a goal orientation. What if you can't ask questions though? What do you do then? Put a copy of Zig Ziglar's goal program on your desk. Keep a Daytimer or planner on your desk with projects marked "completed" for all the world to see as they browse at your desk while walking by. It should be evident to people that you are a goals-oriented person and that you are actively setting and accomplishing goals. Sometimes actions speak louder than words.

It might also be prudent to let people overhear you talking about goals you have met and set on the telephone without making your telephone calls sound like you are bragging to the listener.

Attention to Detail

Do you make sure you have an extra copy of the agenda when you pass a sheet to everyone? "Does everyone have a copy? I have two left if anyone else needs one." You were forward thinking enough to be certain to have copies for everyone and then some. Most people don't do this! Your small actions will communicate volumes to those who you need to impress.

Are you organizing a lunch for the next strategy meeting? Do you make sure that the people who would like vegetarian or special needs meals are taken care of? People notice this kind of detail orientation. What might take an extra minute or two can pay off in a lifetime of dividends. People appreciate other people when they go the extra mile and pay attention to the little things.

When you are left after a meeting with only a few people remaining in the office, go ahead and clean up. Allow yourself to be one of the last people to leave. You even wiped the white board and made a verbal note to fax notes from the meeting to the right people when you got back to your office. Little comments and extras make a good impression.

While paying attention to detail, be certain that the big picture people know that you can drink in the big picture and then really get to the nitty gritty and make things work. Don't bore the big picture people with the details unless they ask first.

Persistence

If you were the parent of a child caught in a burning building, you would figure out a way to get your baby out, and fast. That's what persistence is. Persistence is not doing the same action over and over again and getting the same failure for a result. That is called insanity. Persistence is being able to stick to doing something until it is done right and profitably. Persistence pays.

Communicate to others your ability to persist until you succeed by your non-verbal language (they watch your stick-tuitiveness everyday) and through your admiration of other people who have the traits that you also possess but don't comment on.

"People who stay in the market and just stick with their investment plan typically do far better than those who jump in and jump out all the time."

"Mathematically speaking, persistence will usually pay off, because when you begin to deplete the strategies that do not work, those that do work will eventually surface. I don't know that you have to be a genius to do well in anything in life, but you do have to stick it out until you win."

Your fellow employees and superiors need to hear you talking like a winner talks. Losers speak of failure and giving up. They tried something once and it didn't work. That is why they are losers. You will never be a long run loser because you will persist until you succeed. Although you will never say that to anyone, people will hear your admiration for those who persist, and they will know that group includes you.

Positive Thinking

Some executives like the pollyanna attitude of always keeping a smile on your face, always faking it until you make it. That can be useful in some companies, but not in most companies. A person who is a positive thinker is someone who is not voicing dismal pessimism when a project goes awry. When things go wrong, the positive thinker says, "Huh, something must have gone wrong. We'll have to correct that and get it done right ASAP." It's not so much saying that all bad experiences are lessons and that failure is just another form of feedback. (Tell that to the pilot who crashes into the mountain.) Positive thinking really is the "nothing will stop us" attitude.

Recently Muriel Siebert and Company was rated as the third best discount stockbroker in the country by a major financial magazine. (The company was edged out by Jack White and Waterhouse.) What Siebert did right was to frame all of her new commercials around her company's being ranked third and the pride employees took in that. The only brokerage house on the street headed up by a woman and she was proud to be third among all the big guys! A positive attitude plays well in person and in television commercials!

No one ever has to hear you brag about your positive attitude. No one ever needs to hear your rose-colored vision of how bright things will be someday. What they will hear is how you respond to the curves that life and business throw you. Do the curves last forever or is there light at the end of the tunnel? Do you win in the end or is it over now?

Vision

Do you have the ability to communicate your vision of your future and your company's future to other people in the company? It's always worth being careful when discussing your future with your company, especially when your future vision includes a position that is greatly different from the one you currently have. Imagine that you are in the development division of a company and you constantly are talking about your future in the sales and marketing division. You could be perceived as very dissatisfied with your current position. How do you deal with this paradox?

"Sales and Marketing really needs some creative help. We've been creating the best products in the world and they still are only selling what they did last year. If they don't get it together, I'm going to go over there and really sell our stuff."

"After spending six years developing this software, I'd really love to have a chance to tell the world about it. I've never been so proud of anything we've done here."

"I see this company not just growing and expanding but becoming a driving force in the industry. I think when a lot of other companies in this industry start to taper off, we will be number one because . . ."

"I see myself as helping each department that I come in contact with in the future. I want to invest time here, and later I can see myself moving into marketing and then finance as I mature with this company."

The big idea is for you to be able to see yourself and your company grow, but not appear to be too frustrated or upset with the status quo.

Dollar Management

Do you have what it takes to be prudently frugal? Each dollar spent should promote some greater dollar figure. Some areas of dollar management are difficult to measure, of course. Anyone can calculate the value, cost, or savings of turning lights off at the end of the day or upgrading a PC instead of buying a completely new one. However, how do you calculate the value of attending a seminar or bringing a corporate speaker to your company? What about understanding the value of employee-contentment programs ranging from simple awards and plaques to contests and competitions for cruises or trips? How much are they worth?

Generally speaking, employees who enjoy their work tend to outperform employees who are not happy with their jobs. Employees who are content with their jobs tend to have fewer sick days, a real cost that many people in business overlook. What would happen if you could reduce sick days by 10-50 percent in your company? Did you know that companies that bring in outside trainers and speakers and participate in employee appreciation programs have fewer sick days? What is that worth to a company?

Your ability to communicate your awareness of these concepts in a gentle but firm fashion shows that you understand the value of a dollar. You've no doubt read studies that show that most employees don't just want money, but they want to really enjoy their job. Your ability to communicate your awareness of the obvious dollar-saving and dollar-making strategies shows a basic understanding of what is important to your company. Customer service is necessary. Top quality products are necessary. Yet, the purpose of a profit-making corporation is to make a profit. When you speak of profit in this fashion with those people to whom profits matter, you are going to be at the top very soon.

If you can help the right people see that you came in under budget on your office furnishing cost and find a way to get the extra money back to the general fund you are a recognized winner. Most people spend exactly what they are given. You won't. You are a dollar manager. You'll get a better deal for your company, just as if you were buying a house or a car for your family.

Ongoing Learning

The average employee at work is average. The people who go to the top are people who participate in ongoing learning. They read books, take classes, go to seminars, and become the most knowledgeable people in their company in certain areas, especially people skills. How do you communicate your interest in ongoing learning to people who matter?

"I've always been good in sales. I think spending a day with this speaker will help me learn one or two key distinctions in advanced sales techniques that will turn into one or two sales per quarter. I'd like you to approve this course for me."

"You always say that customer service is the most important part of a company. Lousy customer service is the same as watching your profits go out the door. This two-day course is one that some of the best people from IBM, Microsoft, and Netscape have invested in. I'd like to be able to be as good or better than they are. Can we work it out so I can go?"

Your communication can show that you are interested in constantly learning new information that you can apply in the work place. Learning for learning's sake isn't good enough in corporate America. Learning for profitable application in the work place is what people at the top want to hear about.

Is there a wrong way to communicate about your desire to learn? Sure. You can easily short circuit your efforts by making it appear that you are uneducated or are needy in the area of further education. Always think about what you are going to say before you say it.

The question you will want to ask yourself is this: Do you sound needy, or do you sound like you are going from the top 20 percent to the top 5 percent?

Time Management

Your communication should *not* reveal a time urgency. People who constantly are pressed for time are busy, but it often will appear to others that you are ill prepared or disorganized. However, your communication should reveal that you are busy and that you continue to accomplish all of your important work. As in all communication, your actions and words will determine whether people see you as a winner or as someone on the way down.

One way to deal with people who are at the top, or closer to the top than you are, is to discover what their values are in time management.

"What do you find helps you determine what to do first when pressed between three or four critical projects at one time?"

In this case you don't sound like a rookie asking for advice. You simply are eliciting an expert's strategy for determining the best line of action to take in time management. As with all communication with people at the top, you do not want to appear needy. You want to appear in the top 10 or 20 percent seeking the final clues to the top 5 percent.

Time management is, of course, a vital skill that is not inborn. Time management should be taught to everyone in corporate America. However, it is not, and therefore many people spend their days majoring in minors and working their way down or out of the company. You can be different by learning how to be an effective manager of your work and the clock.

Now you know what the top people in the company are looking for. Let's look at how you can build the specific skills necessary to become a great communicator in your personal and professional life.

CHAPTER 9

Communicating in Intimate Relationships

You are going to sit there until
you have thought about what I've said.
M<small>Y MOM</small>

Women on Top

W<small>OMEN ARE THE RELATIONSHIP-ORIENTED</small> communicators of our species. Men are typically task- and results-oriented people. Women tend to focus on developing relationships and intimate communication with those they care about.

For millenia, men have been dumbfounded by the ways of women and vice versa. The reason of course is simple. Men and women do not think alike. If a woman were to approach a man at a bar and ask the man out for a date without previous communication, the man would almost certainly say yes if he found the woman attractive. This is the way men are. Men are almost honored if they believe that a woman would find them so physically attractive as to ask them out without even knowing what they are like as a person!

Women on the other hand typically find such a request insulting! Women need to feel that a man is interested in them as a person before allowing a positive response by accepting a date. Most women can justify accepting a request for a date if they believe they have earned the respect of the man requesting their presence.

Women prefer to participate in communication where an equal amount of disclosure takes place between them and the other person. When people engage women in communication, those people who share somewhat intimate experiences about themselves tend to be appreciated more.

I teach a class called "Irresistable Attraction" about once per month at various adult education facilities in Minnesota. The class is a one-night experience that allows men and women to learn what it is that members of the opposite sex find attractive about them. Women regularly tell me that they want to develop a relationship of some kind with a man before he asks them out. This relationship (nothing more than a conversation really) could be as short in duration as one hour! Women simply want to be taken seriously. Women know that men do not develop relationships with their buddies just by looking at them and inviting them over to watch a football game. A woman wants to be treated on a similar level that allows her to feel as if the man knows her to some degree before attempting to build a more intimate relationship.

Regardless of your sex, when you are dealing with women, remember that they want mutual disclosure in communication, and that is the normal way of developing a deeper relationship.

Give a Man a Problem to Solve

Men are problem-solving creatures. (We are other kinds of creatures, too, but we are genetically wired to solve problems.) When people talk to men, men go into problem-solving mode. If you want to get a man's attention, then you want to present to him a problem that he can solve. Most women do not understand this male compulsion to solve problems. Women prefer to discuss their problems and share their experiences with no expectation of solutions. In fact, women often feel cheated when a man rapidly offers a solution to a problem or difficulty. With men, the opposite is the case.

Present a man with a challenge and he will communicate with you. He will ask you questions to discover the cause of the problem. He will search with you for the spark that started the fire and then he will put it out . . . and quietly go back into hibernation. Most men are simple creatures, driven by their libido and distracted by their left brain when the desires of their libido are not being met.

Men listen when they believe they can help solve a problem. Men listen when they think what they hear will help them solve a future problem. Men listen when what they hear will in some way make them more productive in some way, for some purpose. Men are collectors of problem-solving tools. Many men have garages filled with screwdrivers, hammers, and saws. Some men have huge libraries of books that have the answers to the world's problems. Still other men have guns, fishing poles, bows and arrows, and knives to solve the problem of feeding the family. If you think of men as being problem solvers, you will be a step up on gaining the attention of the man you want to talk to!

Most men need a self-esteem boost, but you would never know it from looking at them or listening to them. They appear quiet and confident when they are really just being quiet. They *do* tend to solve problems well. Men feel greater self esteem when they are taking charge of a situation and meeting a challenge that they can handle. If you want a man to listen to what you have to say, help raise his SEQ (self-esteem quotient)!

You could help a man raise his self esteem by telling him he is wonderful, good looking, or kind. Those terms are appreciated by all men, even when they aren't true. If you want to communicate with a man, then engage him in activity where his self esteem will be enhanced. Work with him on a project that he is good at.

Have you ever noticed a group of men surround an automobile with an open hood and talk away? There is a problem to be solved and communication comes easy. The man who has his "hood open" (whether he is the hunter, the carpenter, the scientist, the artist) is primed for listening to relevant conversation. He will share his wisdom and listen to reasonable discussion, however tangential.

If you want a man to listen to you, ask him to help you solve a problem.

In the balance of this chapter and the next, you will learn the most common mistakes people make in interpersonal communication. Avoid these mistakes and you will change your life.

MISTAKE #1: One Upping Your Friends: How to Invalidate the Experience of Others

"I'm not listening to you at all, but what I have to say is really important."

Bill: "I had such a bad day today. I got stuck in traffic for over an hour."
John: "That's nothing. I was stuck for two hours."

John just invalidated Bill's experience and cut off rapport and communication, didn't he? How could John have handled this so that Bill would know that he is important to John as a friend and at the same time share his challenging day?

TALKING YOUR WAY TO THE TOP—TIP #1:
Listen Fully Before Sharing a Similar Story

Bill: "I had such a bad day today. I got stuck in traffic for over an hour."

John: "That's terrible. You know they really need to build another lane on the major highways around town. Were you in a hurry to get home, or was it just that you got annoyed because of the pokiness of traffic?"

Bill: "Neither. I had a meeting I had to get to and I was late, so the boss thought that I was putting a low priority on the meeting when really I was racing to get there."

John: "Were you able to explain it to him?"

Bill: "No. There were too many other people around, and excuses are excuses to the boss."

John: "Is it going to affect your job in any way?"

Bill: "Nah, my sales are in the top 10 percent. I just don't like looking bad in front of the whole group. Not really that big a deal."

John: "Understand. Today I was heading home, just for dinner, no meeting or anything, just wanted to get home to Christa and the kids and there was an accident on the off ramp. Traffic was backed up forever . . . but at least I didn't miss a meeting."

In the first scenario, John invalidates Bill's experience in a manner that is typical and common in our culture. This happens every day, and we all have offended others at one time or another. What we want to do to improve our relationships with others is to "get out of ourselves" when talking with those we care about and listen to the concerns and needs of others.

It is almost always best to let someone talk out their problem to the point where it no longer bothers them before we begin to express our needs and interests. The reason is simple. When a person is wrapped up in his own world (what I call internalized), he is going to be almost completely disinterested in what is going on in your world. When a person has been listened to and is able to "get it all out," then the person who was in his own world (internalized) will be able to slowly get out into the real world and feel empathy and concern for others, in this case, you.

The common mistake we all make in communication is trying to communicate two or more messages in one conversation at the same time.

This takes away from mutual understanding and a true concern for the interests of both people. When you let one person disclose all of his feelings and frustrations about some difficulty, he is then far more likely to listen and then care about the difficulties and frustrations you face.

MISTAKE #2: Don't Solve My Problem, Just Listen to Me!

These types of problems in communication are often magnified between men and women. Women often feel the need to express their problems without the absolute necessity of having them solved by someone. They simply want people to listen and empathize. Here are some examples of how men often don't understand women's communication needs:

Jan: "Today was such a bad day at work. The boss yelled at me for not getting copies to all the people at the meeting."
Richard: "No problem. Next time just print out extra copies so you have more than enough for everyone."
Jan: "You don't have to tell me the obvious, Richard. I'm not an idiot."
Richard: "I didn't say you were an idiot. I just said it would be good to have extra copies of all the reports. If you would just think ahead you wouldn't have these problems."
Jan: "I do think ahead, Richard. I didn't know that all of the assistant managers would be there, too. Why do you find it necessary to make me feel stupid all the time?"
Richard: "I'm not trying to make you feel stupid. You could just ask the boss how many people are going to be at the meeting and then prepare for them and a few more."
Jan: "I do check the roster so I know how many people are coming. There was just a miscommunication as to who else would be there. It wasn't like it was my fault."
Richard: "Whatever. I better go cut the lawn." (Leaves)
Jan: (Sits depressed)

TALKING YOUR WAY TO THE TOP—TIP #2: Sometimes Listening Is Better Than Solving Their Problem

Richard and Jan have just had the beginnings of what will likely become a huge argument, and it started over next to nothing. How could Richard have saved the day for his frustrated wife? Listen to the better flow of communication below as Richard realizes the need for Jan to simply share the challenges of her day and not have them solved.

Jan: "Today was such a bad day at work. The boss yelled at me for not getting copies to all the people at the meeting."

Richard: "What happened?"

Jan: "Well the stupid general manager didn't tell me that all the assistant managers were also going to be there, so I ended up looking stupid because I didn't have reports for everyone at the meeting. I was so ticked off, I could have just cried."

Richard: "Did anyone say anything?"

Jan: "Well, there just weren't enough reports for everyone and I felt terrible. It's not like anyone said, 'Oh, Jan, you are such an idiot. It was just that I looked bad. I even called ahead of time to see how many reports I was supposed to bring. I was just so embarrassed."

Richard: "Must've really bummed you out. I'm sure sorry to hear about how unaware some of these people are that you have to deal with."

Jan: "Yeah, they expect you to be God and you just aren't."

Richard: "Well, I don't know about that. You're pretty close in my eyes" (a bit of a grin).

Jan: (a bit of grin and with a playful tone in her voice) "Oh, you . . ."

Happy endings are almost always very easy to accomplish as long as we realize that we want to communicate with people in the manner they wish. Many women share a common trait: They do not want men to solve their problems. They want men to listen to their problems and empathize with them. For men, this concept is foreign. Men are problem-solving creatures by nature. Watch the following scene where Richard really needs help in solving a problem, but this time Jan responds as she would if she were communicating with another woman.

MISTAKE #3: Not Helping Men Solve (Some of) Their Problems

Richard: "The weeds are ridiculously thick in the lawn, the lawn needs to be cut, it needs to be watered, and I just don't have time to do this and the painting, too."

Jan: "Honey, I sure am sorry you have so much work to do. I really understand."

Richard: "Understanding is great but it doesn't paint the house and water the lawn. Can't you at least help me in some way?"

Jan: "Honey, I know you are frustrated."

Richard: "Of course I'm frustrated. There are thirty hours of work to do today and I only have twenty-four to get them done. I'm going nuts."

Jan: "Well, pretty soon it will be winter and there will be less outdoor projects to do."

Richard: "That is so typical. Can't you for once just say, 'Hey, Honey, howzabout I water the lawn for you?'"

Jan: "I just don't understand you. You are always saying I'm lazy. I work my backside off around here for you."

Richard: "Well, what the heck do you think I do for you?"

Jan: "I think that I don't complain half as much as you do, and at least I listen when you have problems. You just go off telling me what to do all the time."

How could this soon-to-be Titanic-like disaster have been avoided? Let's look at the new scene once Jan understands how Richard, and indeed most men, need to be communicated with when they are under stress in trying to solve problems.

TALKING YOUR WAY TO THE TOP—TIP #3:
Gently Help Men Solve Their Problems

Richard: "The weeds are ridiculously thick in the lawn, the lawn needs to be cut, it needs to be watered, and I just don't have time to do this and the painting, too."

Jan: "You're right. That is too much for one person to do. We can do a couple of things. I can water for you after you cut the lawn or we can pay one of the kids on the block twenty dollars to cut the lawn and then water. What do you think we should do?"

Richard: "I don't really know. I hate to pay the money, but I really need a break sometime this weekend."

Jan: "Then forget the money. I'll call the neighbor boy and we will get the lawn cut and watered and that way you can get to paint the house without feeling quite as overwhelmed."

Richard: "Thanks, Honey. Maybe there will actually be time for us then some time today."

Men's and women's communication needs are often very different although they have the same ultimate purpose, which is to experience some sort of happiness or pleasure. The road to happiness and pleasure is paved with talking to people the way they need to be communicated with and not the way we want to be communicated with. When in doubt, the rule of thumb is that women want people to listen to their problems. They want empathy and understanding and appreciation for the experience they are having. They are not looking for solutions to their problems unless they come forward and ask for assistance in seeking solutions.

Men, on the other hand, tend to communicate with the intent of solving problems and participating in goal-directed behavior. They prefer not to participate in communication that "serves no purpose." They often perceive this as a "waste of time."

The exception to this rule happens when men get lost driving, which happens with some regularity. Men do not want assistance in finding their way to and from destinations. So when you find yourself lost with a man, keep it to yourself and act as if little if anything has gone wrong!

CHAPTER 10

Charismatic Communication: Making Other People Right . . . Even When They Are Wrong

The Secrets of Charisma

Now WE CAN FINALLY IDENTIFY the secret recipe for charisma and the ingredients of irresistible attraction! What is it that makes us feel good when we are around certain people? How is it that some people make us feel very good about ourselves when we are near them? So good, in fact that we are drawn irresistibly to them, wanting more. You might think that it is something they are born with or something that they just come by naturally. You may think so because they just clicked with you. More likely it is a result of the way they craft their words, the honesty and integrity in their communication, and the intent that rests at the very core of their thought. When the integrity is there, the words of appreciation, affection, and acceptance flow freely.

Imagine that you are in a discussion with someone and you are having trouble getting your point across. You have explained your point well, but your listener is still feeling lost or confused. You have a choice of making him feel wrong for not understanding, or making him feel good about himself, even though he may be feeling confused and inadequate.

You might say, "I don't know why you don't understand. Let me try to explain it in a way that you can grasp." In that communication you have an intent that makes your listener feel wrong and leaves him feeling even more confused. Even if he is clearly unfocused and wasn't listening, it is still not going to help your position to make him feel bad for not paying attention. You can take this same dilemma and turn it around to your advantage. You say, "Maybe I am not explaining it well" or "Let me make it more clear." Now you have shifted the burden to yourself to explain it in a way that makes no one at fault.

149

Your intention will work for or against you. If your intent is to make someone feel small, stupid, confused, or less in any way, you lose and so does the other person. You may think you emerge victorious when you have one-upped the other person, but in reality you have alienated him and linked some bad feelings to being with you. The more you do this, the more you build a state in that person that is associated with feeling bad. When you put yourself in a superior position, it means that someone has to feel inferior in order for you to feel superior. If a person continually feels inferior around you, they are not going to have any desire to be near you.

On the other hand, *placing a person at ease, helping them feel confident and appreciated, is the magic of great communication.* When you phrase a sentence by placing the burden on yourself, you take the pressure off the listener and, more importantly, you remove any blame or need to make him feel inadequate. This is where your intent becomes very important.

When you are about to enter into an important business conversation or presentation, or when you are enjoying a casual or romantic conversation, set your intention before you begin.

Your words may not be clearly understood, your listener might be distracted or uninterested, or you may be getting frustrated, yet the next thing you say brings your intention right back to center. "You are a very astute business woman, and I can see by your success that you grasp concepts easily. I think I can explain it better like this . . ." Now your listener feels that you are acknowledging her sharp mind, her ability to understand, and you have placed her in a position of wanting to pay attention.

Wendi Friesen recently shared the following story with me. I confess that it really surprised me that someone in this man's position could be such an inept communicator:

> At a sales training session I conducted, the owner of the company had unbelievably poor communication skills, and his best skill was at making his employees feel small and weak. At one point, referring to one of his employees, he said, "The thing that Julie just doesn't understand and probably will never understand is that . . . . In this sentence fragment, in one fell swoop, his intent was clear and to the point. He let her know that she has difficulty understanding things and that he feels she is not smart enough

to learn it in the future. He let her know he had no confidence in her ability to do it differently or for her to grasp whatever it was that he was about to say. You can imagine my delight in the opportunity to find a way to help him understand how his communication might be creating difficulty without making him wrong.

Your intent will help you to begin to shape your words and craft your sentences in a way that will make others feel good around you. When others feel good around you, they like you better, like themselves better, and will want to have whatever it is that you are offering. These principles of intention will create cooperation and harmony, whether you are selling a car, making a romantic connection, or helping an investor decide to trust you with his hard earned $10 million.

Now let's look at Wendi's response to the business owner who had a misguided intent.

Business owner: "The thing that Julie just doesn't understand and probably will never understand is that the customers are usually dishonest."

Wendi: "So, I can see that you are a man who really wants your employees to understand the customers. And you are obviously a man who cares about his employees' needs to get them clear on your point of view."

Now he is not feeling wrong for making her wrong. He is in a position of agreement with me and is receptive to what I will say next. He is also not focused any longer on making Julie wrong. This shift in focus takes the pressure off Julie and forces him to look at his own communication. Now we can explore the ways in which he can help Julie to understand what he really means.

Keep your intention strong, and learn a few phrases that will place your listener in a favorable position, even when he is feeling superior—or, at times, downright vicious.

Helping Your Listener Be Right, Even If He Is Wrong!

Look at these next opening phrases and "make-them-right patterns" that are designed to help make your listener right.

"You are obviously a man/woman who . . ."
    demands the best out of employees
    appreciates quality
    enjoys the finest
    is very astute
    understands how others feel
    catches on quickly
    can spot an opportunity

"One thing I've noticed about you is . . ."
    how insightful you are about others
    how comfortable you are with yourself
    the way you inspire confidence in others
    how quickly you grasp the real meaning of conversation

"I can tell that it is important to you that . . ."
    others see your point of view
    you demand the best in others
    you feel right about making a decision before you jump into it
    you make the most of your leisure time
    others are honest with you

"The thing I've always admired about you is . . ."
    your focus and vision
    how strongly you feel about your decisions
    how direct your communication is
    the way you always say exactly what you mean
    the way you embrace your dreams and hopes

The beginnings of these phrases can help to defuse a difficult moment, shift the intention of the persons you are speaking to, make them feel right and shift their focus inward, no matter what they have said. It also gives you something to respond with when you are faced with a difficult person with whom you need to have rapport. And when you are not with a difficult person, these phrases will enhance rapport and help your listener to feel better around you.

When you are in conversation and you feel the need to be right, take a moment to catch yourself. If you feel this need, it surely means that you will be right at a cost. The high price could be the state of mind of your friend, boss, lover, or child. If you are right, then it can only make your listener wrong. And if your listeners are feeling wrong, they are going to feel bad in your presence. And when they feel bad in your presence, you will be very far from talking your way to the top. So, resist the temptation to make others wrong, even if you are doing it subtly. Talking your way to the top means that others feel better about themselves when they are with you. Talking your way to the top means that others look forward to being with you because they like themselves better as a result of being around you. The way others feel around you is often a result of the words you choose and your intention behind those words.

There are many ways to make other people wrong. You may see yourself in these scenarios and realize that in a subtle way you have been making others feel wrong or bad around you. Some of these scenarios make others feel tense around you. Some raise suspicions. All of them create a negative feeling in your listener and will force them to associate that bad feeling with being with you.

On the other hand, making people feel right, even when they're wrong, is just as easy and far more productive, isn't it?

One of the most charismatic entertainers of the 20th century was Elvis Presley. I'll never forget watching a television interview with Elvis when I was a kid. I didn't know it then, but he never liked war protesters. He served his country and believed that everyone else should. He never shared his opinions on issues like this, however. In the news interview, the woman asked, "What's your opinion of war protesters?"

"I'd just as soon keep my personal views to myself," Elvis replied. "I'm just an entertainer."

"Do you think other entertainers should keep their views to themselves (referring to John Lennon, a big Presley fan, interestingly, and other "peace advocates")?

"No."

It was never Presley's place to make someone else wrong. He wasn't a learned man, nor was he eloquent. He stuttered and was very uncomfortable in front of reporters. He did have one trait that was worthy of note as a communicator: He didn't like to make people wrong.

Knowing what is important to other people is another one of the keys to fundamentally fabulous communication. Therefore when we talk with people and fail to learn about what is important to them, problems will arise!

Eight Habits of Highly Ineffective Communicators

Have you ever been in a conversation where you found your mind drifting, dreaming, and struggling to stay focused? Do you remember how it feels to try to listen as someone drones on and on? When we are faced with a poor communicator, there can be many reasons for the missed connection. Often there are words and phrases that simply shut us down and prevent us from listening as well as we would like. Many times the person communicating is injecting so many negative words and ideas that we begin to feel down and heavy inside. It may just be that the person you are communicating with is boring you because the content of the communication is all about him, about stories you don't care to listen to, and about people you have never met!

What if that poor communicator who is boring you to tears is you? How would you know if you are the one who is inserting negative associations, bringing up insignificant details, droning on about you, you, you? How do you know if someone is really interested in what you have to say, that they are really engaged in the conversation? What is your method of observing whether or not the person or group is interested and intrigued, or tired and looking for the door?

When you become a top-notch communicator, you learn from everyone you talk with. You will notice the subtle cues that tell you if you are in good rapport, speaking in a way that your audience understands, and using words that create desire and interest. You will be willing to identify in yourself those things that push others away and prevent them from listening as well as you would like. This is a very potent aspect of self awareness that allows you to stay fascinating to everyone around you!

In the next section you will look at the areas of communication in which people most commonly go wrong. Presented are eight habits that make for highly ineffective communication. You will discover how you may have been alienating others and forcing them to feel negative when they are around you. As you read these scenarios, decide if you see yourself in them. Take time to be honest about your style of communication and the effects you are having on those around you.

THE ARGUMENTATIVE COMMUNICATOR

Do you enjoy playing the devil's advocate? Are you constantly offering your opposing opinion when it is not asked for? Do you find yourself saying the word "but" often in your conversation with others? You may be an argumentative talker. There is an effective way to take an opposing view, but it may destroy rapport. There is a way to give your opinion, but it may be recieved as unwanted advice. When you continue to oppose the comments of your listener, you run the risk of making him feel wrong, stupid, or uninformed.

THE COMPARISON MAKER

Comparison happens when I share a thought or a feeling with a friend. It might be something that is very personal, or something for which I am looking for understanding. The friend will offer up a response that tells me that she does not really care about what I have to say.

It might go like this: "I have been talking with my boss about how to handle this negotiation with Sally. I tried to get in to see him yesterday, and he acted like he didn't want to talk to me about it."

Friend responds: "I know just what you mean! I had a boss once who was always finding time for everyone else, and everytime I tried to ask a question she would brush me off. Once when George was talking to her, he . . . blah, blah, blah."

If you find yourself always looking to compare an event in your life with one in your friend's life, you can now change this nasty habit and develop the skills of the great communicators!

THE BETTER-THAN TALKER

The difference between a talker and a communicator is clear. The communicator is making an effort at understanding. A talker is someone who rambles endlessly without intending for both people to benefit from the "conversation." The Better-Than Talker is similar to the Comparison Maker, but with a more condescending tone. The Better-Than Talker is not comparing for purposes of being compassionate, but for the purpose of creating superiority. He is interested in feeling superior to the person he is speaking to, and that requires that the listener become inferior. If the listener is feeling inferior, the talker is not in rapport, and any hope for a connection is lost.

THE HEAR-MY-OLD-BAGGAGE COMMUNICATOR

There is a need for sympathy in some people that begs for pity. It may come out of a need to be rescued, or it may be a real cry for help. If you recognize this in yourself, take a look at why you need sympathy from others and why it is important for others to feel pity for you. Maybe you have had a very sad life and you really feel that you deserve a little sympathy. That certainly isn't unreasonable. Maybe you have had the short end of the stick and you feel you really have been a victim of some terribly unfortunate events. That's okay, too. People DO have these experiences. The appropriate place to take this challenge is to a qualified therapist and work through your difficulties with him or her.

With the exception of recent events that demand sharing sympathy (someone losing a job or the death of a loved one, for example), there is little place for running through old baggage in conversation. Old baggage places an obligation on your listener to feel something that he may not want to feel. It also connects being near you with feelings of sadness, need, and despair. The more you do this, the more others associate those feelings with being near you. If you want to help others to feel bad around you, then you should try to get as much pity from them as possible. If you want others to seek you out and feel good around you, then you will want to save the truly difficult experiences of your life for your trained therapist. He can listen with a degree of empathy and objectivity that friends and business associates simply cannot.

THE JUDGMENTAL COMMUNICATOR

When Jason says, "Jim is really getting stressed. He must have some difficult clients right now," it is not a judgment. It is an observation. That's good.

When Cathy responds and says, " I know what you mean. He has never handled stress well. When he blew up at Ken the other day, he was so rude. He can't control himself, and I am really tired of his attitude," that is a judgment. Cathy makes a statement of opinion as to what kind of person he is and how he is wrong for being that way.

If you judge others, you may think that you are doing it to gain rapport or be on their side. You may alienate yourself, however, by showing your lack of self respect. If you are not "internally well aligned with yourself," you may find that you have a need to judge others in order to feel better than they are. (We will talk about effective talking and listening to the self in the closing chapters of the book!)

Speaking judgementally is a dead giveaway to others that you have issues of incompetence and insecurity. Don't play into that trap. Respond in a way that strengthens your position of self respect and self esteem.

In our example, Jason should probably have responded with, "Jim has always been helpful to me. I've learned a lot from him. He has his challenges, like we all do. Maybe he just needs a hand right now."

THE INTERRUPTING COMMUNICATOR

The single most powerful message you can send to your listeners is to use the amazingly simple technique of repeatedly interrupting them. This disastrous mistake is discussed in greater detail elsewhere in this book, but here are a few principles to take note of right here and now. When someone interrupts you, you know that they were not interested in what you had to say. When someone interrupts you, you know that they believe what they have to say is more important than what you have to say. When someone interrupts you, you know they think they are better than you!

When you are communicating with others, take a breath after your partner has finished before you speak. In that breath, you are saying that I heard what you said, I am taking it in, and I am appreciating your communication. This one technique is golden. Not interrupting others could be the single most important skill you learn from this book.

THE COMPLAINING COMMUNICATOR

Complainers face the same trouble as the Baggage Communicators. You feel bad when you are around the complainers. When you complain, the state that you put your listener in is the state that he will associate with being around you. If you are a chronic complainer, you will create negative feelings in others and will push people away, rather than draw them near. Complaining is something best left for customer service and avoided in communication with those you love or with whom you do business.

THE GOSSIPING COMMUNICATOR

Gossip is probably the most evil, deadly, miserable way to communicate. Don't use it, don't participate in it, don't respond to it. You are giving away so much of who you are when you spread or even listen to gossip. As tempting as it is, be bigger than that, starting today. If you are a gossiper, remember that there are others who have evolved beyond gossip. Those people who have risen above the need to gossip see you for what you really are. And here is my take on who you are as a gossiper. You are very insecure, your self esteem is dependent on finding fault in others, your world honors the small, weak, and petty. There is no bond that I would want to share with you by participating in your gossip. I know that anything I tell you will become public knowledge and be used against me.

Seriously evaluate any need you may have to gossip. Find out why it is important for you to talk about others in a way that is demeaning. Notice the reason that you need to spread bad news about others. If you are around someone who gossips, share your thoughts on gossip. When you say, "I really don't want to hear that. It is none of my business. And, anyway, I really like George," you encourage your listener to stop gossiping.

Those are the eight habits of highly ineffective communication. Now let's look at some common mistakes people make in everyday communication.

MISTAKE #4: Ignoring the Values and Beliefs of Others

Miscommunication often happens when we do not consider the personality, the needs, the ideals, the values, or the beliefs of those with whom we are communicating. Discover the makeup of a person's personality—the beliefs, the values, the ideals, the goals, the wants, and the interests—and communication resembles rowing a boat downstream . . . very simple.

TALKING YOUR WAY TO THE TOP—TIP #4:
Learn and Accept Unconditionally the Values and Beliefs of Others

Once we understand what makes another person tick, we can build rapport and enthusiasm within our communication easily. Learning the true values that others hold dear is like having the keys to their soul. Once someone has shared with you his deepest beliefs and values, respect and honor those values.

TALKING YOUR WAY TO THE TOP TIP #5

If you discover people's values (as we discussed in Chapter 3), you can help them get what is most important to them in life!

MISTAKE #6: Arguing with People Who Are Obviously Wrong

Jackie: "I hate parents who let their kids stay up to 10 P.M.

Jane: "What a stupid thing to say. Where did you ever dream that up?"

Jackie: "You always keep your kids up late and have no time for yourselves."

Jane: "That doesn't mean I'm stupid, Jackie. You aren't exactly a perfect mother yourself, you know."

Jackie: "You don't have any rules. You let your kids run the house, and you'll pay the price later."

Jane: "You're just being stupid. We have lots of rules. We simply don't worry about what time our kids go to bed."

Jackie: "Well, maybe you should."

The scene is a familiar one among friends with children. These women have different values about bedtimes and apparently about family rules as well. It's also obvious these two women are close enough to express their opinions to each other. However, they are also at a point in their relationship where the words they use are often cutting and meant to hurt . . . just a little. Here is how words can be transformed from weapons to building blocks for better relationships:

TALKING YOUR WAY TO THE TOP—TIP #6
Hear Out People Who Have
Opinions that Are Obviously Wrong

Jackie: "I hate parents who let their kids stay up to 10 P.M."

Jane: "What do you mean, you hate parents who let their kids stay up until 10 P.M.?"

Jackie: "It's sinful the way some parents don't have adult time. I've always said that there is adult time and there is children's time."

Jane: "Huh, I never thought of that. Is that how your parents were, or did you figure out that this just worked for you guys?"

Jackie: "When I was a kid, we were told that children were meant to be seen and not heard. We weren't allowed to be up after eight o'clock on school nights, and if we were, we would get our backsides paddled."

Jane: "How did you feel about that as a kid?"

Jackie: "I didn't like it then, but I can see the wisdom of my parents. We learned discipline at an early age."

Jane: "What do you think the best part about this is for the kids?"

Jackie: "Jane, they learn that there is adult time and there is children time. It's important for mom and dad to have time together, too."

Jane: "Is that the most important part about late night time together for you guys?"

Jackie: "You bet."

Jane: "Then I think you guys are doing it right. But I wonder whether that is true for all families and circumstances. One thing is for sure, having some adult time would be mighty nice sometimes."

Jackie has decided and has been "programmed" to believe that for children to stay up until 10 P.M. is "sinful." She's obviously wrong. There are instances when it is good and no doubt instances when it is bad, depending on the family and the circumstance.

Notice how Jane defuses the potentially volatile conversation into a non-issue. Whether a family chooses to have adult time or not is really very little reason to attack your friends. Meanwhile, there is no reason for

Jane to argue or fight over an issue about which Jackie is being insensitive. There will come a time when Jane will want to share precisely how insensitive Jackie was, in a very clear manner. However, this is not the appropriate time. This is the time for defusing, not for developing a non-issue into an issue.

We all speak insensitively on occasion. Generally, we speak insensitively when we have been dealt with harshly on the same issue ourselves in the past. If we tend to be overly strict as parents in some circumstances, these are often areas that we had a great deal of resistance to when we were young. When you hear people making bold and obviously foolish statements, don't try to make them see the light of day. They won't when their fuses are lit.

When people cling to strong beliefs regardless of how accurate they are, they will tend to defend these beliefs forever, until death do they, and their belief, part.

MISTAKE #7: Tell Him What to Do with His Money

Consider the following scenario, where a bad financial decision is made because of a foolish belief.

John: "Hey, with that big lump sum you just got from your bonus check, are you going to pay off that 18 percent credit card you've been complaining about for the last few years?"

Richard: "Heck, no. We'll just charge 'em up again like we did last time we paid 'em off and then all that work has gone for nothing. I'm going to stick the money in the bank and keep it safe."

John: "But you'll only get 2 percent in a bank. You will basically get an 18 percent return on your money if you pay off your credit cards, Richard. Think about it. That's a lot of money!"

Richard: "Well, John, when you get your bonus check you pay off your credit cards. We are not going to charge anymore on our cards. They're full, so we can't charge anymore. I'm gonna keep it that way."

John: "But, Richard, that makes no sense. You'll save thousands of dollars if you wipe out the credit card debt!"

Richard: "But in six months we'll have it all back again just like last time. Forget about it, John."

Clearly John is right. Paying off the credit card(s) is a far superior option and gives a substantially better return than the pittance he will get from a bank. The belief he has about charging up his credit cards is legitimate. What has happened in Richard's mind is that he associates charging up the cards again with paying off the balance, and he doesn't want the cards charged up again. So the question is, how can John advise his less financially astute friend without pushing his hot button on credit cards?

TALKING YOUR WAY TO THE TOP—TIP #7:
Use The THEY Technique
Direct People to See the Light
for ThemselvesWithout Hurting Their Feelings

John: "Congratulations on getting the bonus."

Richard: "Thanks, I really worked my backside off to get it this year."

John: "Any plans for my newly wealthy neighbor?"

Richard: "Gonna save it!

John: "Smart man. A lot of people would go blow it on toys or something."

Richard: "Yeah, we've done enough toy buying for a lifetime. It's going to the bank."

John: "Good for you. Hey, whatever happened to that monster credit card debt you had amassed?"

Richard: "Still got it, and that will never happen again either."

John: "Ya' know, Fred's wife tore up all their cards except one they both decided to keep for emergencies. They had amassed about $10,000 in debts, just like you guys, and then they ripped up the cards. Since then, they're still paying 18 percent a year, which is like having $2,000 sucked out of their wallets every twelve months. But at least they aren't digging themselves deeper in debt. Can you imagine? $2,000 per year in interest is $10,000 in five years! In other words, if they pay the minimum payment only, their credit card debt will never go down and they have to work a whole month just to pay the bank. Amazing isn't it?"

Richard: "How do you figure they work a whole month to pay off interest?"

John: "Well, they probably make about $4,000 a month between them, right?"

Richard: "Yeah, sounds right."

John: "Well, if you make $4,000, you have to pay Uncle Sam and the state about $1,000 of that. That leaves you with $3,000, right?

Richard: "Sure."

John: "Well, their minimum payment will be about $250 per month. Maybe a little more. That's another $250 per month, all going to interest. That's $3,000 a year, so they have to work an entire month or maybe a little more just to pay the credit card. Revolting as it seems, they each go to work every day for a month just to pay the credit card. Too bad they didn't have a lump sum like you do to get out of that prison."

Richard: "I never thought of it like that. But if they pay it off, they'll just charge it back up again."

John: "Yeah, they used to be pretty irresponsible with their money, but they made a deal with each other to simply never do it again. And Fred says they haven't. They're going to be hurtin' for awhile for sure, but in the long run, they'll get out of debtors' prison."

Richard: "Maybe we'll get out of jail now. I gotta talk to Janet and see what she thinks."

John: "Good thinkin'. Yeah, now that you mention it, you'd save a fortune and wouldn't have to work for Uncle Sam AND the credit card company anymore . . . just Uncle Sam." (grins)

Richard: "Yeah."

John used a technique that I call the "they technique." This technique is used when you can cite someone else as an example of good or bad behavior and then gently imply, without saying so, how obvious the solution to the problem is. You never directly assert that Richard should or shouldn't do something. You simply tell a story without saying that this is a good solution for Richard as well. It's "just a story."

Using the "they technique" allows you to help your friends and family members in a manner that lets them decide for themselves if they might have a better choice in a given situation. When people are participating in behavior that is obviously wrong or foolish and you want to lead them to a solution that is definitely in their best interest, you can use this technique to help them get what they really want and deserve in life.

Emotional Hot Buttons: Defusing Bombs in Communication

MISTAKE #8: Trying to Use Logic to Defuse a Bomb

Anne: You know, I saw this sign on the road for Planned Parenthood and I thought to myself that is nothing more than planned death. What a disgusting organization.

Chris: Anne, you will never learn that a woman has a right to choose. Why don't you just go blow up all the clinics in the state and become a martyr for your anti-abortion stand?

Anne: No Chris. Not anti-abortion. Pro Life.

Chris: You want women to die in childbirth and couldn't care less how a woman feels when she's been raped and would be forced to carry some criminal's baby. You have no feelings whatsoever toward other people.

Anne: YOU are the one who doesn't care about feelings. Think of that little baby. Who makes her choices? You make me sick.

Few issues are more polarizing than abortion. Anne and Chris have been friends for many years. They take their kids to the park together and they play tennis together, but they disagree on this volatile issue that has no societal right/wrong. It is very personal, and about half of all Americans fall on either side of the debate. How could Chris have handled Anne's outburst differently?

TALKING YOUR WAY TO THE TOP—TIP #8:
Discover How People Came to
Believe in Their "Bomb Issues"
(Religion and Politics, to Name a Couple)

Anne: "You know, I saw this sign on the road for Planned Parenthood and I thought to myself that is nothing more than planned death. What a disgusting organization."

Chris: "Anne, how did you come to think about Planned Parenthood as a disgusting organization?"

Anne: "Because they counsel innocent women to become murderers of their children."

Chris: "I know how strongly you feel about the Pro Life view, and I really respect your feelings about the life of children, especially those that are unborn. In your mind, what they sometimes do may mirror what you just said. Sometimes, though, they help people prevent pregnancy in the first place, which eliminates the choice of having an abortion or not. And I think we both agree that is good, true?"

Anne: "Well, yes, that is true. We both agree that preventing unwanted pregnancy is a good thing. It's what happens after pregnancy that always divides us."

Chris: "You're right, it does. But I want you to know that I respect your point of view, and I know that it is made with sincere love in your heart. I hope someday you'll feel the same about me and my beliefs. Until then, we'll just have to agree on helping women use birth control effectively so there are fewer unwanted pregnancies, period."

Anne: "I still disagree . . . but okay."

Anne's anger has been successfully defused and Chris, through her responsible and insightful communication style, has defused herself, too. No doubt Chris can also debate her own views with anger in her voice. However, instead of creating ill will where none needs to exist, she lets Anne vent her feelings and then find a point of agreement. (These women aren't likely to personally experience an unwanted pregnancy. Why create resentment between friends?)

There is rarely a need for people to make each other wrong and be right themselves. We all have the desire to be right. Over the years we have all been "made wrong" by others many times. Some of us have been made wrong so many times that we feel the need to not only be right but to make sure others know it. Some people even have the need to be right so much that they make others "wrong." These "victories" slowly erode the quality of relationships and make for difficult communication. When a person begins to attack with language, the best defense is often to simply let the person say his piece and then continue on with another topic or issue.

When your beliefs come into conflict with another person's beliefs, there probably is little purpose in attempting to make the other person wrong and yourself right. Simply let the person share his belief with you. Try to understand how that belief was created. What experiences led the person to this belief? Learn what creates beliefs in the people you talk with. Be gentle. Be respectful. Be curious and be tolerant. These are all traits of good communicators and people who communicate with love.

Emotions are at the core of any human behavior. As you watch people act and react every day, you will notice certain patterns of behavior. People tend to display the same emotional responses week after week, month after month, and year after year. Emotions are a part of people that do not readily change.

CHAPTER 11

Secrets of Love and Intimacy

Love is acceptance without judgment.

Communication with a special person or persons is going to play a large role in the quality of your human existence. It's possible that the most wonderful experience you can have on this planet is being involved in a romantic relationship.

When you fall in love with someone, there is a euphoria that is rarely ever matched in terms of quality of experience. When you "fall in love" with someone, you are also often blinded to many of that person's faults or negative behaviors. This can be good or bad, depending upon how the relationship emerges and grows. Unconditional love is acceptance without judgment. That is both a reality and a goal. It is a spiritual concept that is challenging to manifest in physical form. As the relationship does grow, the problems your lover has kept silent about eventually surface and you become aware that there will need to be "work" in the relationship. What makes the love bond grow deeper is that upon the revelation of the faults and problems of the other person, we still love that person and appreciate his or her ongoing love for us despite all of our problems and faults. Lasting love can be euphoric, but really it is identified by its acceptance and lack of judgment.

In this chapter let's start at the "beginning." If you are currently unmarried or are "unspoken for," and wish to be married or spoken for, now you will see just how to realize that desire. You are about to discover the very simple way that successful relationships begin. If you are currently married or spoken for, this chapter will help you turn the difficulties of your current relationship into the seeds of a happy and fulfilling experience.

Who Are You Looking for?

People who are in a "good" relationship knew at one time just what they were "looking for" in a relationship. It may have been conscious or unconscious. The criteria may have been physical, emotional, mental, or spiritual (or some combination of these four), but they did know. They knew what kind of person they wanted to find. In some cases, they knew exactly which person they wanted to emerge with!

When beginning their search for a love partner, many people look "out there" and hope to find someone, and they wonder why the person of their dreams isn't there. One problem is now in place that cannot be immediately overcome. When someone is looking for *any* another person, it has the same effect as looking for no one. No sense of attraction is emanating. When people begin "looking for" specific traits or features, whether physical, emotional, mental, or spiritual, there is a magnetic-like filtering process that attracts the people their way. By analogy, if you go driving in rush hour just hoping to see the "right automobile" for your next purchase, you will see nothing. If, on the other hand, you decide to look for a specific car, you will see dozens of them on your way to work. This is similar to the experience we have all had of purchasing a car and then seeing dozens of them on the road. What happens is that a part of our brain now recognizes the new vehicle as significant to the self. You identify with it.

The very same mental process helps us recognize the people with whom we want to invest in relationships. Unfortunately, many people don't isolate the key traits of the individuals with whom they want to forge relationships. If one determines the characteristics of the people he wants to build relationships with, his internal processes will screen out the people who don't meet these criteria and will filter in the appropriate potential relationship partners.

If you are in the "looking" stage (and we are all looking for some kinds of relationships most of the time) then just what kind of person(s) are you looking for? We all need to engage in relationships that will help us grow as people. This means we need to be with people who share some similarities with us and some significant differences. People need to complement each other as well.

Some people are good with money. Others are not. Two people who are not good with money in one relationship could be a recipe for failure if a solution isn't found. Many people can't stand the sound of a crying child.

Others find it to be just another noise that kids make. If two people who can't stand the sound of crying children marry, what happens?

How can we attract the right people into our space? How can we spot the people we really want and need from the masses? We must have some knowledge of what needs we want met and what we have to offer others. Many people haven't thought about the characteristics they are looking for in other people. Those who are looking for certain traits, behaviors, and characteristics tend to find what they are looking for. You can thank the miraculous construction and functioning of your brain for this!

Exercise: If you are in the looking stage for a partner, write down the key physical, emotional, mental, and spiritual traits you will be looking for in that person. Be certain to include everything that you think of. If your partner needs to make a lot of money or you don't want to pursue the relationship, write it down. There are no wrong characteristics to include.

Having seriously evaluated what you are looking for in a special person on all levels allows your brain to begin filtering out people who don't match your criteria. This is a very important function for your brain because it makes the task of discovering possible life partners simple. The brain knows whom you are looking for and will now do the work for you.

In all relationships there is a sense of give and take. There is a certain unwritten scoreboard of contributions to the relationship that are unconsciously evaluated by each person. When both people contribute fairly equally to the relationship, the relationship is generally happy and content. When one person contributes far more to the relationship than the other, the relationship will probably end or be very unhappy.

Exercise: You have recorded those characteristics and traits that you would like to see in a potential partner. Now it is time to put the spotlight on you. What do you bring to the relationship for the other person?

What benefits, experiences, and resources will a person gain from you?

What do you see as your physical, mental, emotional, and spiritual strengths? Write down all that you will invest into this soon-to-come relationship.

Exercise: Now comes the hard part. What inherent problems do you bring into a relationship with a life partner? (Are you in debt? Are you outside this person's religious faith? Are you obese? Are you unhealthy? Do you have an unstable career or no savings?) Write down all of the areas you are deficient in. Be as thorough and honest with yourself as you possibly can be.

Exercise: For each item that you listed as a deficiency, once again note the item in writing and then explain to yourself what you plan to do to correct this deficiency. If it is impossible to change, simply write that fact next to the item.

Exercise: Having now taken an honest and penetrating look at yourself, once again turn your attention to your potential life partner descriptors in the first exercise. Some of the notations you made were wants and some of them were "must haves." In this exercise, you must answer the following question: "If the person had everything else I wanted except_____, would I be happy with this person?" Answer this in response to each characteristic that you noted in the first exercise above.

Circle each characteristic for which you offer a "NO" response. These are your MUST HAVE responses.

Obviously the MUST responses begin to limit the people with whom you are interested in sharing your life. Therefore you must be completely honest and true to yourself. It is not shallow to want someone who is good looking, or wealthy, or even have a high degree of education. The question you want to answer for yourself is, is this really a MUST HAVE? If someone has a history of sexual abuse or has committed murder, those may be MUST NOT HAVE traits.

You have now carefully discovered what you truly want and need in a love relationship. Your brain will screen in potential applicants. Similarly, as other people go through their day-to-day life, you will be screened in and out by them as well. This is a very important process to understand and appreciate. We cannot take "personally" the fact that we do or do not fit into someone else's life plans. This process is one that most people go through on some level (conscious or unconscious, and occasionally at the spiritual level). When two possible life partners meet each other, there is usually a "click" shortly thereafter. This "click" is the "this is the one for me" response. The person may actually be only one of many, but when you feel the click, the experience is often one of "love at first sight."

Intimacy:
Creating and Re-Creating Deep Bonds of Love

Intimacy should not be confused with sex, even though it is true that we are often emotionally most intimate with people with whom we share our sexuality. Being intimate with someone is being completely open and authentic with them. It means that you are you and the other person is who he or she is. There are few if any hidden agendas or secrets in the intimate moments. For the purpose of this book, we will only talk about the intimacy that occurs in romantic relationships and marriages.

If you are married, the "bond of marriage" may sound like a prison, or it may sound like a special kind of "oneness." The Bible alludes to the idea of two becoming one. This is the bond we will consider in the balance of this chapter.

Half of all marriages end in divorce. In half of the remaining marriages, the people are unhappy. Those marriages that are successful have several common characteristics, one of which is good communication. This means that the participants are able to express their feelings in a relatively open manner. This doesn't mean that there will be no fights or arguments. On the contrary, complaining, fighting, and arguing will happen in the best of marriages. *Complaining, fighting, and arguing are, in fact, symptomatic of potentially good marriages.* These people are communicating, and that is a fundamental necessity to a deeper and more intimate relationship.

Almost all marriages and intimate relationships need "work." The question is how can you work on a relationship? It seems pretty intangible when you read the sentence on paper, but in real life it really is a workable process and it begins and ends with communicating.

Marriage and relationship partners tend to be similar to one of our parents in some ways, or they tend to fill a need or desire that one of our parents was unable to fill when we were children.

The following exercises will help you discover some interesting secrets about yourself. Take your time as you answer the following:

1. List several things you most admired or loved about your father.

2. List several things your father did or said that hurt you or caused you pain.

3. List several things you admired or loved about your mother.

4. List several things your mother did or said that hurt you or caused you pain.

5. What elements of admiration, love, hurt, and pain do you find in your current partner that you also found in your parents?

Dr. Harville Haddix has discovered that we often marry someone who at the unconscious level filled the void left by a parent. In other words, sometimes we tend to marry someone who is similar to one of our parents in order to complete our childhood. This isn't a conscious act, of course. Our unconscious mind is like a magnet that attracts what it needs. In this important aspect of life, the unconscious mind wants whatever person is needed to fulfill childhood.

For this reason and others, you thoughtfully determined just what traits and characteristics you are looking for in a partner. This was a conscious exercise. If you are already involved in a relationship, then answer this question to determine if you may have married to complete your childhood:

"When you first chose your partner, was it because of a powerful romantic inclination toward him/her?"

If the answer is "no," then you probably didn't marry to fulfill an unconscious need for completing childhood. If the answer was "yes," then you may have done just that! (Neither answer implies a successful or failed marriage in the end. It is important to be aware of just how and why we have engaged in the relationships that we have.)

For our purposes, let's assume you answered "yes." If you answered "no," skip ahead to the Successful Relationship Elicitation section below.

Because you married in part to complete your childhood, you can probably predict that your partner has many of the qualities you need to complete your self and be whole.

Think about your partner for a moment and see for yourself if they don't have strengths where you are weak. Your partner also may be weak where you have strengths. This does not mean that you are in a dysfunctional relationship. In fact, it can be a recipe for lifelong happiness and success! It does mean that you have a conscious call to action because you may now know why your marriage isn't moving forward as happily as you would like. This marriage often finds its partners asking, "Why did I ever marry him?" "What did I ever see in her?" "How could I have been so stupid?"

The time to cut off the problems that are coming is NOW. The problems that appear in these marriages often seem to be minor to those watching from the outside. For you, however, they will be utterly terrorizing at times. Little things will cause huge blowups. These are signs of the unfinished childhood discussed earlier. Why? Because your partner is triggering the childhood arguments and punishments you experienced as a child with your parents. You are almost yelling at your parent(s) as you yell at your partner.

The very best promise that we can make as partners to insure a better relationship is this: "I promise to stop criticizing and start listening to my partner." Criticism is what the parent did to you that created the wounds that you experience to this day. This doesn't mean that mom and dad didn't love you. They probably did. They probably were simply insensitive to your feelings and needs. It is not important in this context to understand why the parent criticized and hurt you but to realize that criticism is a relationship destroyer. Criticism is like pouring salt on those wounds after they have been reopened. Criticism will destroy the bond of love between two people.

Persistent criticism is a plea for the relationship to end.

Partners who are unconsciously attempting to complete their childhood tend to argue, fight, and bicker a great deal. This is to be expected, as this is what happened when you were a child with your parents! The pain is much deeper than one would expect, another indicator of an incomplete childhood.

The Mathematics of Happy Relationships

Partners who are completing their childhood can now do so with this new awareness in mind. They can grow more deeply in love and sometimes fall deeper in love all over again! One way to have that special someone fall deeper in love with you is very simple. Increase the number of positive experiences with each other. It sounds easy but according to Dr. John Gottman, if your relationship is to be truly happy and long-lasting, your positive moments will need to outnumber your negative moments five to one. In his brilliant book *Why Marriages Succeed or Fail,* he suggests that negative moments are fine and part of reality, but that the positive moments need to outweigh the negative ones. This is one of Gottman's keys to success in marriage. You will need to begin thinking about how to experience five times as much positive interaction time with your partner.

Beware of Hostility

Hostility is attacking someone verbally with the intent to do harm. Some people simply fly off the handle and criticize people. As discussed earlier, that has to be stopped. Others will complain about the behavior of their partners. That isn't so bad in the long run, though it isn't exactly a recipe for happiness. What is among the worst sins detrimental to the soul is communication with the intent to harm, whether in public or private.

If you or your partner intentionally communicate with the intent to harm, you must stop it immediately. Hostility is something that no soul should be involved in. There is no benefit from hostility for anyone. The desire to harm others through communication is a sign of serious relationship problems that need to be corrected as soon as possible.

If your partner is intentionally communicating with you in a hostile manner, you need to gently share this information with him at the first reasonable moment. The partner should be allowed to communicate his feelings about the reason for his hostility and then move to a solution. The solution is not the silent treatment but rather increased communication. However, as you deal with the specific issue of hostility, do not bring up all the relationship problems of the past. This only gives cause to do the exact opposite of your goal.

What model of communication would you propose? Propose it. Get agreement if appropriate and start communicating with the intention of making each feel good about the other. The exercises on the coming pages will help you rebuild a relationship that was on treacherous ground.

Re-Creating Love in Relationships

Will the marriage end or will love be re-created? If it's time to start over, do so now. The following plan for re-creating your relationship will be of great help. Here's how:

1) Design a completely safe environment in which you and your partner can communicate.

If you have been striking your spouse, change your behavior. Changing your emotions will happen later, but change your behavior now! Your spouse may have been hit as a child. If you tend to blow up at your loved one, stop now. He or she probably was yelled at as a child. If you get up and leave when you are angry, stop it now. Perhaps your spouse was abandoned as a child, and you're acting just like the parent. Think carefully about these examples before moving on to number two. Create an atmosphere where it is safe to talk and communicate. Promise each other that this is a time to listen and not judge or evaluate or point fingers. Create an atmosphere where you can experience positive communication.

2) Describe three things that you can implement in your marriage today to create a safe environment for you and your partner to communicate.

3) Stop all criticism immediately!

There is no such thing as constructive criticism to the parts of the unconscious mind that are attempting to finish their childhood!

4) Create sessions of healing acceptance.

Healing acceptance sessions occur when you and your partner sit down and talk just as if you had been hit by a car in an accident. You want to find out if the other person is all right and see what you can do for him. You need to tell your partner that you want him to acknowledge what you are about to tell him without rebuttal or explanation on his part. No defensiveness is necessary. You are simply telling him that you are wounded and that it hurts. You will not blame him. You will use statements such as "I feel . . ." and "I hurt . . ." He should say, "I understand" and "What else do you want to tell me?" "Go on." "Okay." Those four statements and questions are the sum of what the non-injured partner should say.

It is vitally important to never attack your partner during these "healing acceptance" sessions. Keep it open and loving, and then your marriage will be on its way forward!

5) Perform random acts of kindness for your partner.

Bring a card or gift home after work. A small and inexpensive gift shows your thoughtfulness and can do wonders for your relationship. Notice the key word is "random." It means "unpredictable." Be unpredictable with your times of giving.

Do something that you normally don't do around the house. If you never wash the dishes, do them one night. If you never cut the lawn, do it. The unexpected can be very pleasant and very appreciated.

6) Return to a successful dating ritual you liked.

Was there something special you did while you were dating? Do it now.

7) Express your love and feelings for your partner with hugs, kisses, and verbal affirmations of love, and do it often.

Most people need to be hugged and kissed. Leo Buscaglia used to prescribe at least a dozen hugs per day for the maintenance of a relationship. Saying, "I love you" may get old after 30,000 recitations but you never hear of anyone complaining that their partner tells them that they love them too often!

8) Discover your needs and wants while sharing yours.

For you to have a wonderful relationship, discover what your partner currently loves about your relationship. Then ask your partner what he thinks could improve your relationship. Ask your partner the questions below, in the Successful Relationship Elicitation exercise. (Don't do this all in one sitting!) This exercise will help you discover what is important to your partner and will help you transform your relationship.

Successful Relationship Elicitation

The following questions are to be used as discovery tools for you and your partner to learn more about each other and deepen your bond. Use these questions as tools to gently start to help you and your partner "peel each other's onions." The first questions will help you and your partner build resources to which you can refer in tough times. Later questions help discover weaknesses and areas that can use change or improvement. Spend about twenty minutes for each partner on these questions over several days.

What do you love most about our relationship?

What is the next best thing about our relationship?

After that, what is the next best thing about our relationship?

What else?

What do you believe you should learn about me to improve our relationship?

What do you think I should learn about you to improve our relationship?

What are two things I do that annoy you?

What are two things you do that you think annoy me?

How happy are you with our sex life?

What can I do to make our sex life more intoxicating?

What would you be willing to do to make our sex life more intoxicating?

When we argue from now on, should we agree to kiss and make up before the argument gets out of hand?

What will our "cue" be for this to happen?

What do you do around the house that you think I don't appreciate?

What do you do at work that you think I don't appreciate?

What do I do that you probably don't appreciate as much as you could?

What do you want to know about my past that I haven't told you?

What do you want me to know about your past that you haven't told me?

When should I be jealous?

When do you think you should be jealous?

How can we go from having a good relationship to having a fantastic relationship?

All of these questions allow us to discover more about our partner in a couple of hours than we may have discovered in years. Questions are an under used element of communication in our culture. Beginning to ask gentle questions will put you on the track to improving communication and thereby improving your relationship, no matter how good or bad it already is. Learning what is important to your partner and being certain your partner understands what you need and want makes having a good relationship much easier. You take the guesswork out of knowing what helps the other person feel more at ease with you.

What other questions would you like to ask your partner?

Relationship Troubleshooting Strategy

Relationships can occasionally take a downturn, and the cause may be elusive. An argument may go unresolved, even though you have learned what it takes to have a successful relationship. In such a case we search for what is known as a triangle.

A triangle is created by the inclusion of a third person who has been creating a negative influence on one of the people in the relationship. This person is often an instigator. The third person is often a "friend" of one of the people in the relationship and sometimes may not realize the damage he or she is doing to the relationship. The instigator most likely has failed in his/her relationships and has now taken it upon himself to advise. This person can be very damaging to your relationship and can be dealt with as discussed in Chapter 12, "Talking to Well-Intentioned Dragons."

In order to discover who the Well-Intentioned Dragon is, you will need to sit down with your partner and ask, "Who is influencing us to argue?" The search might take some serious thinking. If two names come up as instigators, then there are two triangles. Once you have discovered the negative ideas and their source, you can take action. Cutting off communication with this person is probably not necessary, but changing the content of communication with the person probably is.

CHAPTER 12

Talking to
Well-Intentioned Dragons

W E HAD TO TALK ABOUT IT sooner or later, didn't we? Not everyone we know and love is interested in using his or her life for the creation of happiness in their own life and the lives of others. Sometimes people do want to do good for others but instead impose their own beliefs and attitudes on others, thereby violating the principal definition of love, which is acceptance without judgment. Those people who sincerely would like you to do better or achieve more but hurt you with their words and actions are what I call Well-Intentioned Dragons. They mean well, but their mouths can spit fire and produce immense amounts of harm.

This person stands in contrast to the Dragon, who harms you emotionally and sometimes physically, with full intention to do so. The Dragon needs help and not the kind that you can give. You can still love the Dragon, but you, by yourself, will not likely be able to change him or her.

The Well-Intentioned Dragon sometimes knows his words often cut to your soul and hurt you. Still, most of the time, he does mean well and probably even "loves" you. The Well-Intentioned Dragon is a person who is probably worth salvaging as a friend or lover, if you are already in the relationship. A person with good intentions is worth talking to.

How do you recognize Well-Intentioned Dragons? First of all, they hurt you emotionally, knowingly or not. Their advice is free. They seem to have a clear handle on your life, money, and relationships, yet have not fared well for themselves. In most cases, they are acting from their best intentions. This person can be a lover, a relative, a business partner, or any friend.

You decided long ago to put up with the Well-Intentioned Dragon. Unfortunately, this is not the person who is going to help you in your spiritual growth and share with you the deeper experiences of this life. Most dragons have been advising you for years. No matter what their experience, they know better than you in most, if not all, areas of life. The dragon read about your problem in the recent issue of a tabloid magazine or saw an expert on a television talk show. The dragon is going to fix you . . . for your own good . . . whether you like it or not. Many people have numerous Well-Intentioned Dragons running their lives for them. The more dragons in your life, the more energy you use in non-constructive communication.

How have you dealt with these people in the past?

You've probably tried to argue with them, and that strategy failed. At some time or another you probably pretended to listen to them, nodding at appropriate times, but they demanded your agreement and constantly check to see if you are following their advice. Whatever you eventually did probably didn't please the Well-Intentioned one.

The Well-Intentioned Dragon can only be dealt with on his own level. You will never succeed in trying to prove yourself to the dragon, so do not try. The dragon really wants control of your life because his life is out of control. You need to control your own life so your goal will be to re-focus the dragon's thinking. This sounds easier than it normally plays out in real life. Consider the following example of dealing with the well-intentioned one.

Imagine that you want to purchase a new car. The Well-Intentioned Dragon wants you to buy a different car than you would like to buy. Most people who have relationships with the Well-Intentioned Dragon argue with him (or her). Not anymore. Instead, in our automotive dispute we will offer this line of thinking to our friend:

"I've been thinking the same thing you have. It does make sense to buy a used car for a lot of reasons. They can have lower payments, less depreciation, and are broken in. Would you do me a favor and research which cars are the best used cars out there. I don't want to make a bad decision and screw up."

One of two things will happen. The dragon may research the cars for you, which may actually prove productive. If so, the person will come back with new information, which you will promise to study. If he does not wish to research the cars for you, then say this:

"No problem. I know someone who has had great luck buying cars. I'll check with him to see what the best cars are before buying a new or a used one. Thanks for your thoughts." (Never say "advice" to any dragon.)

Regardless of what the person says next, you say, "Yes, I'll check it out." Then change the subject to something he has going on in his life, such as, "Oh, did you ever replace that broken dryer?"

If the subject is not buying something, you can use the same strategy. Here is another example of the strategy that will work in your daily dealings with various kinds of dragons:

W.I. Dragon: "You know, the kids really should be going to bed much earlier than 9 P.M. on a school night. You are messing up their body rhythms."

You: "That's really interesting that you mention that. I've been thinking about that lately. Would you look into that for me and find some research articles about body rhythms so I can learn about it?"

W.I. Dragon: "I just know because that's how I grew up, and it always worked for me."

You: "That makes sense. Well, if you get the articles, I'd love to read all about body rhythms and do the right thing. It's something I haven't studied and obviously should. And speaking of rhythms, how's your broken dryer doing?"

The reason we talk to the Well-Intentioned Dragon is because we love them. We desperately want them to change their ways and communicate in a more loving manner. They may never change, but we can at least create a tolerable communication environment.

The Communication Formula
to Defuse W.I. Dragon's Heat

1) A dragon gives you advice.
2) Agree with the dragon that it is an interesting subject.
3) Tell the dragon you'd like to learn more about it.
4) Ask him to send you information or research articles.
5) Change the subject to something going on in his life.

Write down the names of five Well-Intentioned Dragons in your life.

Write down how you feel about each of these Well-Intentioned Dragons.

When will you begin dealing with each these dragons?

Flame-Throwing Dragons

Not all dragons are well intentioned. Some of the people you communicate with may want you to fail in some or all aspects of life. The Well-Intentioned Dragon believes he has your best interests at heart. He wants you to do well. He simply hurts you emotionally as he tries to do so. The Flame-Throwing Dragon, on the other hand, throws flames with the intent to hurt.

How could any soul want to create harm for his "brothers and sisters?" It is hard to understand all the motivations. Some people suffer from severe mental illness. Some people simply have suffered so much in life that they now turn their anger on those they work with or love. Whatever the reason, you really must remember that fire is fire regardless of the reason they are throwing flames.

It is important to be with people who uplift you and help you find happiness and love. A rule of thumb that might be worth considering is that it's best to encourage positive relationships with those we are connected to. People who are attempting to harm you emotionally, physically, and/or spiritually are not moving you forward within your life purpose and mission. Instead, they are a drain on your emotions, your physical well being, and your spiritual nature.

> *Flame-Throwing Dragons drain your physical, emotional, and spiritual energy.*

These dragons must be gently confronted with the truth. Attempting to alter the focus of a Flame-Throwing Dragon is generally ineffective. More direct action is necessary.

Portrait of a Typical Flame-Throwing Dragon

1) They tend to take pleasure in bringing you bad news.

2) They tend to alter neutral or positive news and put a negative slant on it as they communicate with you.

3) They tend not to keep their word or promises.

4) The people they associate with tend to have lifestyles that are unhealthy or breed trouble.

5) They tend to make small problems appear large.

6) They tend not to respect their own property.

7) They tend not to appreciate the good that is done for them.

Who are the Flame-Throwing Dragons in your life?

What are some of the characteristics of these less than friendly dragons in your life?

How would you like to deal with each of these dragons in your life?

Talking to Flame-Throwing Dragons

When you see that someone is constantly leaving you with bad feelings and negative emotions, that is a sign that you may be dealing with a flame thrower. When a person possesses a number of the above traits, there are two reasonable ways to deal with him. Confrontation is certainly the best of the two options we will discuss below.

Confrontation. Confronting anyone about anything is rarely a pleasant task. When you decide to confront the Flame-Throwing Dragon, you will use questions as your first approach:

1) How will you decide when it is time to let me move ahead with my life in the direction I need to go, even if I am wrong?

2) What will you do differently from now on to assure that we both respect each other's directions in life, even though we have fundamental disagreements?

3) What benefit would you gain if you continued to hurt my feelings and I was not able to continue spending time with you? Is it worth it to you to let go and let me be me?

4) Will you allow me to make mistakes in my life that will not kill me? I know you believe I'm going in the wrong direction, but it will not cost anyone's life. So, unless you sense physical harm, will you allow me to make the mistakes that I will learn from?

Cut off Communication. This choice is obviously a last-straw decision. It means that the Flame-Throwing Dragon in your life is not respecting you or your wishes. Therefore you will cut off communication with him until he changes his perspective about you. There is no benefit for either you or the dragon to continue communicating if the dragon is not willing to grant you the freedom to be you. You allow others to pursue their own course, regardless of your estimation of its value. Those who will not afford you the same respect may have to be cut off at the source. With luck, the person may return someday, interested in participating in a caring relationship with you.

You might tell him this: "You need to know it is sad that I must say this. I've chosen to "X" in my life, and you have refused to let me be me. I care about you as a person. I always will. But I need to be responsible for my own life. I ask nothing of you, except that someday you return, knowing that I will be here, when you sincerely want me to be me. That day will be a wonderful day. For now though, I cannot contribute to your happiness because you want me in bondage to your wishes. I cannot allow that *and* become a responsible human being. So until we meet when you wish to set me free in your mind, I wish you well."

You can communicate these thoughts in any manner you wish. It's very important that you be very precise when stating your point of view. Your hope is that the person will return shortly with the willingness to grant you "beingness" and accept you for who you are and what you do. This is your final avenue in dealing with the Flame-Throwing Dragon.

It is never our desire to stop talking to people. Ideally, we want to have the best communication lines possible with everyone we meet and care for. You will never throw flames at others, of course, and we will always practice accepting others without judgment. When encountering the dragons in your life, remember that ultimately they will affect your emotions, your spirituality, your physical well being, as well as that of your family and the rest of those you love.

Love is acceptance without interpretation.

Acceptance means that you grant "beingness" to those in your environment. We can define "beingness" as pure acceptance and the absence of judgment of yourself and others. You allow someone to be who they are and not who you would like them to be. Interpretation can mean to evaluate, to judge, or to attempt to alter in some way. To accept someone without interpretation means that you grant people beingness without attempting to improve, judge, or change who they are. Acceptance is similar to unconditional love in philosophy. Love truly is not something that is conditional in nature. Love is acceptance unconditionally given.

In the space below, write down the names of those who love you without obligation, requirement, or judgment.

How can you express your appreciation to these people?

As this day moves on and the weeks pass by, consider this truth of loving others unconditionally and accepting people for who they want to be and not who you want them to be. Observe yourself and how you feel inside when you stop passing judgment on those you care about. Watch how this simple snapshot of reality can alter your perceptions of everything and everyone around you. As you begin to grant people beingness over the coming months, notice how many more people begin to grant you the same respect, admiration, and love.

By filling your life with the people who support your efforts and goals, you'll discover how much easier it is to move forward in your life. By granting beingness to others you uncover happiness within yourself that you never knew was there.

CHAPTER 13

To Thine Own Self Be True: The Key to Life-Long Success and Prosperity

Now it is time to find out what our nature is and how to move toward being your most authentic self possible.

Wisdom, ethics, and kindness are three legs of a triangle that complete and perfectly complement each other. The individual with wisdom who experiences giving kindness and ethical behavior is prepared to touch many lives in a truly wonderful manner. No one will be wise, kind, and ethical in all their daily activities overnight. As we strive toward this tripartite ideal, we become more real and experience our true selves as we really are.

The Kind Communicator

A person's intentions generally will come through in their communication once good communication skills are learned and practiced.

The New Testament says that love is patient, charitable, and kind. Kindness in part comes from acceptance without judgment. Kindness is a natural extension and outgrowth of love. It can be nurtured, however, through practice in acting kindly toward others, thereby cultivating the love that remained hidden. Kindness is found in the authentic self.

If there were a measure for kindness, what would your Kindness Quotient be?

Do you find yourself being truly helpful to others without promoting your own agenda in the meantime?

Do you find it easy to listen without interrupting?

Do you ask others about themselves before talking about yourself?

Do you bend down to eye level with the children you talk to?

Do you pay a compliment when you can?

Do you find it easy to do nice things for others?

Do you smile at people to let them know you are "happy" with them?

Do you speak in a kind tone of voice when communicating with others?

Do you avoid criticizing others?

Do you work out your anger with the appropriate person and not the innocent bystander?

Do you help people feel at ease?

Are you able to give to those less fortunate than you?

Do you remember people's names and greet them by name when you see them?

The "yes" response, while appropriate in answering the above questions, is one that you might want to go back and reconsider before moving ahead in this chapter. Regardless of your responses, today you can begin to touch your authentic self by practicing kindness with everyone with whom you come in contact.

The Ethical Individual

How important is it to do the right thing? *To the self, being ethical and authentic is the only way to "be."* When someone "does the wrong thing," the unconscious mind does a number on the person. Like your inner self, your unconscious mind wants you to do the right thing (as it perceives it to be right) and will help you feel very guilty if you do the wrong thing. When you do too much of the wrong thing, the unconscious mind will give you signals through pain, physical symptoms, emotional symptoms of anxiety, depression, panic attacks, and all kinds of other somatics. This doesn't mean that if you experience anxiety that it was you, your inner self, that caused the anxiety, but it does mean that your unconscious mind is giving you a conscious signal that something is wrong, regardless of whether the self or the external environment stimulated the symptom.

Your real and true self is "closer" to the unconscious mind than the conscious mind. This doesn't mean that the unconscious mind is kinder or gentler than the conscious mind, however. The unconscious mind is simply a collection of all of your experiences and memories, your pains and joys. The unconscious mind drives your behavior toward that which we want and need and away from that we don't want or need. The unconscious mind, for better or worse, is the goal-seeking part of the individual. The unconscious mind always wants to achieve the goal. Your true self, on the other hand, wants to do the right thing. Sometimes the two come into conflict. When they do, the unconscious mind will direct the human unless there is a "conscious mind intervention."

The unconscious is not bad or evil. It is simply the part of us that directs our goal seeking behavior, good and bad. Without the unconscious mind, we couldn't drive and chew gum at the same time. The unconscious is filled with all the behavioral patterns that we have ever experienced. That means that our unconscious mind drives the car to work. That is why we often don't remember anything that happened on the way. We can be lost with thoughts of the day or problems or dreams as we drive to work, and the conscious mind attends to the problems and dreams. Meanwhile, the unconscious mind directs the car to work. It's really quite amazing when you think about it.

Exercise for the Ethical Person. Invest one day in a self-ethics course. This course is free of charge and you will design it yourself. As people talk to you, regardless of the subject or content, determine whether or not what you are about to say is going to help or harm the person. As you go through the day, pay close attention to the feedback you receive both verbally and non-verbally from each person with whom you come in contact. Record the responses to your communication throughout the day while each communication is fresh in your mind. At the end of the day, evaluate your level of intentional and purposeful kindness. At any point did you accidentally create harm for someone? How can you change this in the future?

The Wise Soul

Napoleon Hill, the greatest success philosopher of all time, said that each of us has access to infinite intelligence. That means that except for the biological constraints you have within you, you can attain great insights, knowledge, and wisdom. Wisdom, however, is more than being knowledgeable. Wisdom is about doing that which is right. Wisdom is about being aware of how your actions and words affect those near to you. Wisdom is being able to see the trappings of life and becoming aware of how to avoid the pitfalls along the way. Wisdom is recognizing that cause and effect are alive and well. What you sow you reap. When you say or do something, it can come back to haunt you or embrace you. (Sometimes sowing and reaping is a farm-like process: Planting takes place in the spring. Harvesting comes long after, in the autumn.)

> *Wisdom is knowing what the right things to do and say are, then saying and doing them.*

> *Wisdom is knowing that your thoughts shape your experience.*

Some time today, maybe even now, allow yourself to go inside and say "hello." Smile at the fact that you are talking to yourself. You spend all day talking to other people's selves and now you can listen to yourself. Sit quietly. As other thoughts enter your mind, acknowledge them then allow them to fade. Listen for the silence. If any worry or problem enters in, simply allow it to fade. Listen to the silence. Take five or ten minutes to listen to yourself and just be silent. See how good it makes you feel. You are touching your soul.

People at the Top Live Life on Purpose and with Good Intentions

We really are here to be happy. We are also here to do and be something unique and special. What is the purpose of your life? The goal of this chapter is to help you find the specific purpose and path for your self to take in this life. I have no idea what that is for you, but I can share with you a map that will help you on your way.

Your purpose in life is central to who you are as a human being. People who live the happiest lives have more than a sense of purpose. They live their purpose intentionally. When you are living your life intentionally, with purpose, you will have all of the richness that life has to offer. Living with purpose means being involved with the people you care about most in life. Your purpose is a reflection of the true you.

Goal setting as a practice is an important part of life, as you learned earlier in this book. Most people participate in goal setting outside of living their major life purpose. When goal setting is done outside of your core passion, it only breeds frustration and mental agony. This chapter helps you discover your life purpose and how to get on your life's path once and for all. Your life's purpose and mission, if you will, are discoverable by asking yourself some important questions you can answer below.

The Discovery of Purpose

It's possible that your life purpose will change as you evolve. If you have truly searched yourself for the answers to these questions, you can see that your place here, on this planet, is important. It appears that we have a far greater impact within our own lives than we ever imagined. The reason is that we *are* here for a reason! We have the ability to experience and greatly alter our present and future. You have the ability to detach from the irrelevant things in life and direct yourself in the direction in which you are meant to be moving.

As you move through your life each day, you may become frustrated on occasion. At these times you can highlight this thought in your mind:

> *Everything that exists was originally a thought.*

Purpose Starts with Thought

As you look around you, you discover that everything that is, was first a thought! There are no exceptions, are there? This is certainly a startling revelation the first time most people consider it. Look at an object in the room. How long was it from the time "they" first thought of the "thing" to the actual realization of the thing? Everything was first a thought. Nothing that exists had any other origin than in a thought.

We are what we think.
All that we are arises from our thoughts.
With our thoughts we make the world.
Speak or act with an impure mind
and trouble will follow you.

Speak or act with a pure mind
and happiness will follow you.

Buddha

Look around your environment. If you live in a free country, your environment is largely a product of your thinking. If you live in a beautiful environment, that says something about your thoughts, doesn't it? When you realize that many of the beliefs you were handed when you were a child were limiting, you will probably reevaluate them. Usually these limiting beliefs hold us back from authentic relationships because we are afraid. Today we can begin to change that.

Beliefs are often like second-hand clothes. We get them from our parents and those we grew up with. These generally well-intentioned people told us what to believe, and we did just that, without critical examination or consideration. In fact, it was necessary to believe our parents as we needed a framework to "work" within. Now we are adults and we can reevaluate all of our "given" beliefs and change our lives instead of continuing with "hand me down" thinking.

Go "inside" and let's do a brief exercise about finding your purpose in life.

1) What are some people, places, or things that you would like to have in your life that you currently do not?

2) List some people, places, and/or things you would like to meet, go to, or get out of your life.

3) What is currently holding you back from having what you need to fulfill your life purposes?

4) What is currently preventing you from eliminating the unwanted elements in your life?

5) What positive purpose is served by each of the negative elements in your life? Answer this question carefully.

Frequently we gloss over the secondary reasons why we keep negative things in our life. Example: You have an illness. You would rather be healthy, but a part of you is experiencing a secondary gain. Secondary gain can be sympathy or money or compensation, getting out of work, or any number of possibilities. By identifying the secondary gain, you can truly discover how to eliminate the negatives in your life. The reason is simple. Once you know what the various parts of your mind want for you, you can then "negotiate" with yourself to make sure that you still get the good things it intends for you without all of the terrible negative baggage that is currently included.

Our beliefs have landed us squarely where we are today. Whatever mental patterns we were acting upon in the past have probably not helped us accomplish that which we are here for. You will not fulfill your purpose if you do not believe you will.

Almost everything a person is and does has a direct cause and effect relationship with his or her future beliefs. Therefore it is absolutely vital to design a new set of beliefs that will allow you to realize your true potential for living life to its fullest. It took some time for reality to catch up with your beliefs as they are today, and now it will take a little more time for your newly designed reality to catch up with your new beliefs.

We tend to fulfill most true beliefs that we have about ourselves. If we think we will get something, we normally will. When what we want is someone else (as in an intimate partner), remember that conflicting plans and thoughts will not always find a workable composite plan! In things that are solely personal in nature, one tends to realize his beliefs and thoughts.

Most of the "things" in your environment were desired by you at one time, which is probably why they are in your environment. That sounds simple, but it is profound! Your eternal reality caught up with your beliefs! Did you buy groceries this week? Undoubtedly. You needed to have a belief that you were going to actually get those groceries before you created a plan to get them. If someone told you, "You can't have groceries," you would likely laugh at them (or worse). When you really want or need something, the need tends to be realized.

How to Talk to Youself

There was a time not so many thousand years ago when the spoken word was considered magic. The Bible discusses the use of language in conjunction with faith and belief in a manner that is consistent with effective intrapersonal communication.

If you are going to be authentic with yourself, you cannot be filling your mind with lies as many "self talk experts" will tell you to do (though maybe not in those words!). Talking to yourself in a truly effective manner has three components. First, you will say something to yourself. Second, you have a belief that it will become a reality. Third, you will take some actions to make the thought reality. One of Jesus' life purposes was to heal the sick. I want you to look at some of the communication patterns he encouraged and shed light on two thousand years ago.

When Jesus healed a blind man, note the reason Jesus gave.

Jesus: "What do you want me to do for you?"
Man: "Lord, that I may receive my sight."
Jesus: "Receive your sight; your faith has saved you."

What saved the man was his own faith! As you consider your life purpose(s), remember that they will come to fruition as the thoughts are believed with certitude and acted upon in faith.

James, the brother of Jesus, explained how to gain wisdom. He told the readers of his letter to do the following:

> But let him ask in faith, with no doubting, for he who doubts is like a wave of the sea driven and tossed by the wind. For let not that man suppose that he will receive anything from the Lord; he is a double-minded man, unstable in all his ways.

The above quote indicates that James taught that doubt would impede any chances of succeeding in your objectives, your life purpose. You can't just fake it until you make it. See your real life purpose(s) and know that you will succeed in doing what you are here to do. Doubt is the mother of fear, and once fear enters the intentional life, a person becomes paralyzed (emotionally and mentally).

Doubt creates fear. Fear creates mental, emotional, and spiritual paralysis.

Have confidence that everything you see was first a thought. Know that when there is an intentional purpose, results happen. Faith, certainty, and expectation play a key role in achieving your life purpose(s). Therefore, when you are talking to yourself, you should allow no sense of doubt to enter into your mind as it relates to your purpose. If we are to fulfill the purpose of our life, then there is no room for doubt. Where there is doubt or fear intermixed with faith and belief, a paradox is revealed . . . and nothing much else.

When you communicate to that part of you that is "the most true you," you must remember that you are talking to the real you, the part of you that is interconnected with the fabric of the universe. Essentially, we need to learn to be on the same wavelength as the universe! That may sound complicated (and it would take a book to explain it), but it amounts to keeping your conscious mind in tune with who you really are. Therefore, we must go back to the purposes for your life in this chapter and act and talk in a fashion that is consistent with the established reason for your being here.

What to Say when You Talk to Yourself

1) Make statements of expectancy to yourself. These statements are certain and knowledge-based statements that something *is,* something that we do not yet see. In other words, you know that thought precedes manifestation, therefore accept the "thought as the thing."

2) Make statements to yourself knowing that the words imply the manifestation process has begun.

3) Make statements in the present tense. What you need is stated in the present tense.

4) Be truthful with yourself.

These four keys to effective communication with yourself allow you to realize the proven power that is within you to manifest thought into physical reality. There is always a part of you that doubts success, but the part that is sure does not doubt that some "thing" will be manifested that was once thought. Somewhere deep inside of you this part also knows that the process is not "magical." There will be a followup of some kind on your part to bring the thoughts you have into reality.

How long will it take for results to begin? How long will it be before the manifestation of reality takes place from the time of thought?

The answer is very simple. When all four keys are met, the solution will be met. The realization will be met. The realization could take one second, one year, or a century. Interestingly, many people who have used some form of self-communication in the past have believed that they only need to believe to manifest. What they forgot was that *doing* goes along with the manifestation. Edison, Bell, Ford, and all the great inventors didn't simply "think" of their inventions. They conceived the ideas for their inventions and then worked to manifest them. They believed in their thoughts so much that they dedicated their lives to their thoughts. They were authentic.

A farmer can plant seeds, and know they will grow until harvest time. If the farmer cares for his crop, waters his field, and ultimately harvests his crop, he realizes his objective. This is precisely how it is with the purposes you have discovered for your life. With all of this clearly understood, here are some sentences that you can use to meditate on or use as a kind of mantra. Certainly you can use, and should use, your own personal communication for your specific life purposes.

1) I learn more about my life purpose every day.
2) Each day I live more purposefully.
3) Today I am in love with life.
4) Today I like myself.
5) I make positive changes in the world.
6) I give more of me to those I love.
7) I now perceive problems as challenges.
8) I consciously decide how to use my time.
9) I happily am responsible for my life.
10) Today, I am the person I choose to be.
11) I know that the world would be a different place if I were not here.
12) I consciously decide what I will think about.
13) I find it easy to move toward the realization of my thoughts.
14) I am mentally creating a healthier body today.
15) It is becoming clear how my life is able to manifest my life purpose.

There are several ways that you can use mantras or self talk. First, you can take one thought or sentence and repeat it dozens of times throughout the day. Another method is to create messages of manifestation on paper, then put them on audio cassette tape and listen to them regularly, perhaps at bedtime. Still another method is to write out your self talk, then read it to yourself, silently or aloud, three times each day as meditation.

Self talk becomes imprinted only as it is linked with emotion. Therefore it is best to match each statement with the proper emotion. If you want a passionate belief imprinted, state the meditation passionately.

If at any time there arises an internal conflict in reading your meditations, it is important that we create a happy resolution to the internal conflict you are experiencing. In order to be "internally aligned," you must integrate the "parts" of you that are not currently in alignment with "you" on your life mission. Almost everyone needs to make alterations if they are going to be successful in fulfilling their life purpose.

Internal Dialogue

Internal dialogue is the sum of all the talking that goes on inside of you. Internal dialogue should be composed of productive "discussion." Unfortunately, we often discover that as we read a meditation or state a need, a part inside "wakes up" and rejects the idea. For example: Imagine you are beginning a weight-loss program and you say to yourself as part of a meditation program, "I see myself becoming twenty pounds lighter." Now, imagine that a "part" of you says, "No way do I see myself twenty pounds lighter. I've been this weight all my life!" This is called incongruency.

The goal of internal dialogue is to resolve this paradox. This is precisely why most self-talk programs and affirmation tapes simply do not work. *When there is incongruency, no change will be made and no manifestation will occur. Affirmations alone will not overcome incongruency.*

The following internal dialogue resolution pattern will help you establish a productive internal dialogue and will make you more "whole and integrated" as a being. Whenever these incongruencies come to consciousness, you can deal with the incongruencies easily, as long as you use the general pattern that follows.

Internal Dialogue Problem-Resolution Pattern

1) "Will the part of me that doesn't want to lose weight (or whatever the internal disagreement revolves around) tell me why that is? It's important for me to have me focused on my purpose."

2) The part tells you why it doesn't want to lose weight.

3) "What positive intention does that allow you to accomplish?"

4) The part tells you what positive intention or benefit it is doing for "you."

5) "First, I'd like to thank you. I appreciate that. Would it be okay from now on to still help me get the positive intention and help me lose weight by_____?"

(Fill in the blank with how the part can get what it wants and you can attain your objective. As long as the part gets its positive intention, it will agree to your request.)

6) The part agrees.

7) "Thank you. Let me know if I ever seem to be letting you down."

This is of course a very simple outline of self therapy. Many variables can come into the mix that are not accounted for in this pattern. If you run into problems I simply suggest you contact a hypnotherapist who is experienced in ego state therapy, also known as parts therapy. These kinds of incongruencies are important to resolve because you want to be an integrated whole person. There is nothing wrong and everything good about talking to yourself!

Talk to Yourself with Optimism

For many years it was thought that talking to yourself positively would in and of itself cause you to create change and get the results you wanted. The notion probably would have worked if it were not for the negative life patterns most of humanity received as a child. Before you begin to improve upon the negative patterns that have long been imprinted in your behavior, it will greatly help you to be able to recognize the common patterns. Once you are able to identify negatively imprinted patterns, you will be skilled in ceasing negative thinking.

Credit for the development of workable optimism patterns needs to be given to Martin Seligman, psychologist and author of *Learned Optimism.* Seligman discovered that it is possible to overcome negative patterns of pessimism by mentally disputing your current patterns.

Negative Programming Patterns

1. PERSISTENT NEGATIVE PATTERNS

Frequently you may notice that there are areas of your life in which you believe problems will continue. These patterns are called helplessness patterns because your internal dialogue tells you that there is nothing that you can do to get out of the current state, so you might as well not even bother trying. Helplessness is a learned condition. Helplessness generally begins in childhood, when a child's behavior is squelched or the child is told that he "can't do anything right." Helplessness is also created when a child believes the universally unqualified statements that are made about him. These include: "You are a complete idiot." "You will never learn." "You are irresponsible." "You don't use your head." "You can't do anything right."

Helplessness can be created physically when a person is locked in a room and not allowed to come out. When something like this first occurs, a child will scream and kick and fight for his freedom. As time goes by, the child will stop fighting and realize he is helpless. What seems to be discipline on the parent's part is really the creation of helplessness in the child. Similarly, a child who is stopped from doing something over and over will eventually give up and never try to do it again. When this form of helplessness generalizes, it can become a universal belief about themselves, and they will be helpless in other areas of their life.

All of these things return daily in life in the form of negative internal dialogue which constantly reinforces the beliefs that have been created.

In the space provided on the next page, please note some of the people who successfully taught you to be helpless in certain areas of your life, regardless of their intention.

What were some of the specific events, words, or methods these people used to teach you that you were going to be helpless in these areas?

2. PATTERNS OF CAUSE AND EFFECT

When a child feels that negative events are his fault, even though these traumatic or terrible events occurring in his or her environment in no way are caused by the individual, there is normally a generalization of cause and effect. The child believes that he caused the effect. The child believes that he caused the events to happen. An example of this would be the child who is born into a poor family who believes that because he is unable to work, the family remains poor. He may also believe that it is his fault that his parents do not get along, as he is always in the way.

Many situations of "false responsibility" occur in a child's life. These situations can lead to semi-permanent false beliefs about the individual's cause and effect over external events.

In the space below, note at least three events that happened in your past that you believed were your fault but that really were not.

How did each of these events create a sense of false responsibility about similar events that happened later and may still be impacting you today?

3. PERVASIVE NEGATIVE PATTERNS

How often have you heard someone (or even yourself) say, "I just can't do anything right!" This usually follows a failure or perceived failure of one specific task. This kind of negative pattern is pervasive in nature. The inability to accomplish a single task becomes generalized to "everything and anything." Other pervasive negative patterns are those that generalize specific actions or people to an entire set of actions or people. One bad teacher comes to mean all teachers are bad. One boring book generalizes to all books are boring.

In the space below, note at least three generalizations you have made that were triggered because of one specific action, person, or negative experience.

In the space below, note at least three generalizations your parents have expressed that seem to have no evidence to support them. Write down how and why they became generalizations (beliefs).

Which of these generalizations did you adopt without careful evaluation?

All of these negative patterns are with you all of the time. They emerge in your internal dialogue. Normally, these beliefs, these generalizations, go unchallenged in your mind. The patterns are accepted and "normal." When there is an internal argument between belief structures (parts), it simply means that you hold two points of view on one subject. An example:

"On the other hand, I think Democrats care more about people. Of course, Republicans don't want to spend my hard-earned money. I don't know who to vote for."

This kind of internal dialogue is healthy and typical of conflicting beliefs. You simply have two generalizations in opposition to each other. Unfortunately, this very simple problem can create very complicated challenges that are rarely resolved. Procrastination is one such problem.

Procrastination can stop the authentic life cold. Procrastination must be conquered. Procrastination is the result of incongruency. Once you are aligned with your purpose in life, you do not procrastinate. Procrastination therefore only happens when there is conflict internally. Someone who is living "on purpose" and is in touch with their inner self doesn't procrastinate, because the next step is clear. This is a key reason that manifestation happens with people who are on purpose and often doesn't with people who are incongruent.

Talk to Yourself to Eliminate Negative Patterns

Affirmations will not overcome powerful negative imprint patterns in the mind. The affirmations would simply be rejected as lies. The internal problem resolutions pattern can be effective, but that is best done with a partner, and a partner is not always available. The disputational model that you will find below seems to work remarkably well in most cases. You must talk to yourself using non-negative-thinking language to forge new beliefs that will help you live on purpose.

The Disputational Model

1. IDENTIFY THE ADVERSITY

What specifically is the current problem you are experiencing? You are not going to clear the feelings involved that have come down from similar experiences. You are simply going to challenge the limiting belief that is being voiced in your self talk. You are going to dispute the limiting belief now, and later on you can use the internal dialogue resolution pattern to clear up the emotional impact so similar problems don't come up over and over again in the future.

Identify the adversity. Example: Your boss yelled at you and you feel terrible because he must just hate you. He must be thinking of firing you. That is what your internal dialogue is telling you.

2. BELIEF IDENTIFICATION

The adversity is that your boss yelled at you and you felt terrible. The belief that your internal dialogue created for you was that he hates you and is thinking of firing you.

3. CONSEQUENCE

You started thinking of getting another job, losing complete focus on the task you were doing. You became stranded in thought. You got nothing done for the rest of the day. Tomorrow could be even worse.

Stop here and think about what has happened up until now. Something bad happened, a belief was generalized, and the consequences were not good. This is where people who do not live on purpose stop thinking. Their internal dialogue has spoken and that is the "final word" on the actual adversity. The next step is the key to overcoming these adversities and accomplishing the work that needs to be accomplished.

4. DISPUTATION

You now debate with the part that decided that your boss hated you. "That's ridiculous. My boss doesn't hate me. He was probably just in a bad mood today because we didn't meet our sales quota for last month. I was the first person he saw and he blew up. There's no reason to feel terrible." You are disputing your original interpretation of the event. You are effectively arguing your conclusion with yourself.

5. ENERGIZATION

You cannot simply leave the debate in a stalemate. You now create a plan that makes sense to your entire self.

"So anyway, yes, he yelled at me, but if I were to be upset by that, then I'd get as much done today as he will, which means nothing. If I do nothing today, *then* he'd have a real reason to be upset with me. Therefore I'll do my work even in trying circumstances. Anybody who would fire someone like that, doesn't deserve me working for them!"

Then you work! The negative stimulus of being yelled at doesn't imprint or generalize into procrastination because you have effectively talked to yourself! Rather, the negative event becomes a *trigger to get work done and be an effective member of the sales team.*

This is what living on purpose and talking things out with yourself can do to change your life. You gain control of who you are and your emotional responses to the events of daily life. This allows you to live on purpose and be who you are instead of an effect created by your environmental factors around you.

Most people hear their internal monologue and dialogue. They also tend to forget that their initial internal dialogue is not the final word in what is the best course of action in any given situation. Effective self communication is critical to living on purpose. Knowing what to say when you talk to yourself is truly a wonderful gift. As you have seen, how you talk to yourself when negative events happen can change your life.

Being authentic with yourself means being real and genuine. You probably can't simply open up with each and every person you meet immediately. There is a game, a play we have chosen to live out, that demands foreplay before more intimate and deeper communication. During romantic foreplay, we create enhanced arousal so the final acts and climaxes are more powerful. The same can be said of talking with ourselves and others. This book has given you the true secrets of communication, happiness, love, and talking your way to the top. In the next chapter we will put the fundamental principles of communication together into a framework of actually outlining your map and mission statement for the life you want to live.

CHAPTER 14

The Map to the Top:
Your Personal Mission Statement

EVERY GREAT BUSINESS HAS A MISSION STATEMENT. That is the statement that is communicated clearly to every employee that goes to work for that company. A mission statement puts everything else that a company does into context, and it sets criteria by which the company can judge its performance. A few years ago, Stephen Covey, the author of *The Seven Habits of Highly Effective People,* brought the critical element of a corporate mission statement to the individual. The concept has been a grand success! Napoleon Hill originated this idea long ago when he had people write down their "definite major purpose" on paper and constantly revise the definite major purpose each day of their lives.

The idea is to create a context for your life so you are, as Zig Ziglar often says, "a meaningful specific and not a wandering generality." Indeed! When you live your life in the context of specific ideals, goals, and values, you tend to be more focused and thoughtful about your daily work and play. In this chapter you get the opportunity to place the framework for all of the people skills you have learned up to this point. If you do the exercises in this chapter, you will have rounded out the skills that take people to the pinnacle of success!

You know how to communicate effectively now. The next step is to actually gain a vision of your future and to write your mission statement for your life. Your mission is central to who you are as a person and to your effectiveness as a communicator. The most successful, fulfilling lives all have more than just a sense of mastery of communication skills. These people live with passion. They live as if they are ON a mission. They are living a wonderful daily journey with a sense of purpose, a purpose that is natural and comfortable.

When you are on a mission, nothing can stop you. Being on a mission means engaging yourself in those activities that are most important to you in life. Being on a mission means being involved with the people you care most for in life. Your mission is a reflection of the true you.

Goal setting is an important element of ascending to the top of every ladder in life. We must strive to be better lovers, better parents, better business people. After all, it's pretty easy just to sit back and live an impotent life, isn't it? It is interesting and a bit unfortunate that goal setting is usually done outside the greater context of a life mission. This only provides frustration for the individual. In creating a personally fulfilling life we utilize goals within the framework of a personal mission statement. In other words, if goals that you set are not compatible with your mission statement, then you can make new goals.

Your mission in life is discoverable by asking some important questions of yourself.

Drawing Your Map

Please answer the following questions in the spaces given below. You may use extra paper if necessary. Without the benefit of the "discovery session" that follows, please answer in some detail these next two questions.

What is the purpose of your life?

If you do not know, what would you like the purpose of your life to be?

Next, select up to four major purposes for your life. It is very important that you write your own mission, not someone's distorted image of you. Your life mission can be as simple as being a good parent and spouse or as encompassing as being a worldwide evangelist to save souls. Or both!

Note your mission(s) in order of importance to you. THIS IS VERY IMPORTANT. Your true mission is that which you will not compromise for anything. Circle your most important life mission if you write more than one. Do this below, now, before you read any further.

Life purpose and life mission are similar concepts. The work you have done above will help you hone in on your personal life mission below. (The author's personal life mission is to continue to create a life for my family that is full of love and happiness. My secondary mission is to free the minds and hearts of people across the globe, to help people learn to dream and realize their dreams.)

Knowing your life mission is a very powerful and sobering discovery.

Your life mission is the purpose and the reason for which you are alive. No one can tell you what your life mission is. You and only you can discover your mission(s) in life. Many people go through their entire lives without ever uncovering their mission in life.

Once you know what your mission is in life, the mission YOU have selected for yourself, then you can write a personal life mission statement. Your personal mission statement will include the following points and possibly more that you feel are necessary. Simply complete the sentences below with your first response. If two responses immediately come to mind, note them both. Please do this now, before proceeding.

The reason I am here, alive today, is to:

My mission in life is to:

I will be the best me I can when I:

What gives my life a true sense of meaning is:

More than anything in life, I want to be:

In addition to those five key areas, we can also consider some of the other elements of ourselves before constructing our mission statement.

What are my greatest strengths?

What do others feel my greatest strengths are?

If I could do anything in life and not worry about money, what would it be?

What characteristics do I like most in other people?

What (and/or who) makes me feel happy inside? Why?

What is most important to me in life?

If I could change the world, what things would I change?

What are my greatest talents, skills, and abilities?

Who am I most important to in life? Who else?

Before I die, I want to accomplish the following:

Before I die, I want to do the following:

My most important values are:
(Among the myriad of values, a few are listed below to spur your thinking.)

love	friendship
peace	stability
joy	wisdom

happiness	knowledge
independence	serenity
security	passion
adventure	health
fitness	courage
sex	intimacy

(Many people confuse values with beliefs. Beliefs are not values. Beliefs follow values. Beliefs are accepted truths we hold about ourselves and the world around us. Some beliefs are limiting in nature, while others are valuable for personal growth. We will discuss beliefs and values in much greater depth later.)

My most important values, in order, are:

Detailing the Map to the Top

Now you are ready to design the first draft of your personal life-mission statement. A mission statement can be any length. It also should be noted that you will probably alter your mission statement. And when you read this book again, you will be given all the keys to design your life and take you to the top! Many events occur in life that warrant a redesigning of our lives. As we design and later redesign our lives, it is important to be certain that who we truly are is a mirror image or our stated mission in life.

Being on a mission points you in a general direction in life. Your life has a physical beginning and a physical ending. These two events can be marked as points on graph paper. The space between these two points is your time line. All other events in your life occur between these two points. Some people use arrows on the ends of their time lines to connote something similar to the concept of an eternal soul or spiritual life before and/or after physical life.

It allows you to have the arrow on a piece of paper as a metaphor that represents the direction we are headed in life. The endless arrow can represent our "time line." This line will then allow us to place goals that we want to achieve in the future as part of our mission. The arrow reminds us that goals are not an end, but stops along the way on the time line of life.

Use all of the personal information above to write your personal life-mission statement. The space available below is where you will want to write this first draft. If you need extra space use a separate sheet of paper. This is your first draft only. After reading the entire book, you will write another life-mission statement.

My Life-Mission Statement

Now that you have written your mission statement, be certain it truly represents your thoughts, wishes, and desires and not those of others. So many of us live our lives to please others. Helping others be happy is noble. Living to please others is not noble. And it is not a path for happiness. It does not allow for a life for which you are the designer, and therefore you will not be happy.

Once a mission statement is in print, you have the ability to imagine that all the points on your life line are going to be an important part of your life mission. Problems will arise. These are problems that need to be overcome and are critical to understanding your life mission. Setting goals that are congruent with your life mission is also a necessary and important facet to designing your future.

The time line below represents your life from the present, the beginning point of your personal life-mission statement, and moves toward an infinite "end." You'll also notice that we anticipate problems, and we anticipate the accomplishment of our goals as we move into the future.

TIME LINE

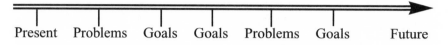

Present   Problems   Goals   Goals   Problems   Goals   Future

As you can see, a life line has problems and goals along the way. Life is not simply about achieving goals. In fact, a life of living to fulfill goals is not any more fulfilling than a life of overcoming problems. A great deal of our lives is spent solving problems. What kinds of problems occur in life that we can assume will happen along the way?

People we love will die.
People we love will grow to dislike us.
People we care for will get hurt and face great problems.
We will have financial setbacks on the way to financial stability.
We will have accidents occur in life that we will be unprepared for.
People we care for will become ill.
We will become ill.

There are many more problems and traumas that will occur unexpectedly, and some will often appear to be placed unfairly before us. Some problems have easy solutions. Others are much more difficult. We will always face problems head on and never bury our head in the sand in hopes that they will go away. In addition to problems, we will have goals that we set and achieve. After each goal in life, there will be more problems to be solved and more goals to be achieved. Achieving goals will never stop, nor will working to overcome life's problems.

As we prepare to design our lives, we can take into account the need to ready ourselves for setbacks. Those who are prepared will survive! Those who survive can achieve.

Achievement is the fulfillment of goals, purposes, and missions. Achievement of a life mission is not the absence of problems. There is never an absence of problems in life. In fact, if there were no problems in life, there would be no achievement.

Now that we have a basic understanding of our life mission, we have provided an "easel" for the design of our life. We have a sense of direction of where we are going in life. Now it is helpful to give the reminder that our life-mission statement can be revised at any time. Always stay on top of your life so you can keep focused on what is important to you.

CHAPTER 15

How One Famous
Radio Talk Show Host
Talked His Way to the Top

I LOVE SUCCESS STORIES. Whenever I hear about someone who went from zero to one million it makes me feel good inside. I know that the American dream is still alive! I asked my good friend Wendi Friesen to interview Tom Sullivan and find out how a boy with nothing became a young man worth millions of dollars. What role did his ability to communicate play in his success? What is there to learn from his success and experience? After Wendi introduces Tom below, she will interview him. The interview took place in his lavish twenty-fifth-floor office in downtown Sacramento, California. Occasionally I will break into the interview to make some comments. I will make these comments in brackets to highlight certain key elements of this dialogue that will change all of our lives!

Tom Sullivan comes to mind as a most powerful communicator, doesn't he? He has the communication skills that have allowed him to literally talk his way to the top. He started out in the real world as a highway patrolman and is now a highly influential financial expert heading up Everen Securities in California. He has a top-rated radio talk show with KFBK in the Northern California area. Tom took over Rush Limbaugh's microphone when Rush left KFBK. Those were big shoes to fill, and Tom has done it beautifully. One thing that strikes me is his ability to communicate clearly, easily, and in a way that people understand. He is a man you feel comfortable being with. In his presence you sense his sincerity, and it comes through in every word he says.

He rose from an upbringing where he thought being poor was the only lifestyle there was. He is now very successful, influential,

215

and one of the nicest guys you would ever want to meet. He has risen to this level of success because of his excellent communication skills. I would like to share with you his experience of becoming a powerful communicator.

Here are the verbatim transcripts of my interview with Tom offering his insightful thoughts on talking your way to the top.

Wendi. From where you came from as a highway patrolman to where you are now must have been the result of some great communication skills. Where did you learn to communicate well?

Tom. Well, one of the things about talking is that as a highway patrolman you have to be a good talker. You really are dealing with somebody's ego. You are taking a complete stranger and telling him you have made a mistake, and I am now going to hand you punishment. It is very hard for us to accept our mistakes and have someone point them out so bluntly to us.

W. Did you have some skills as a highway patrolman that worked well for you?

T. Yes! There is always someone bigger than you, no matter how big you are. And they may be drunk. A highway patrolman needs better communication skills than just about anybody. Today the height standards are gone, and you have all types of officers from all backgrounds. You need now, more than ever, if you are ready to bring them to jail, for people to cooperate with you.

W. What would you say is your most valuable skill or gift in communicating?

T. Well, that is why I raised my eyebrows when you sat down and asked me how I talked my way to the top, because I had no formal communications training. I don't think about how I do whatever it is that I do. It is just the way I do things naturally. I never knew what I wanted to do, I never had this pre-planned, pre-programmed idea of what I wanted to do. I just punt every day of my life!

{Notice the "earthiness" of Mr. Sullivan's communication. See how well he puts us at ease? He is just like us. Simple. This is a typical trait of people who are well liked.}

W. While some of it is genetic, there is a way that you learned to become a great communicator, perhaps someone who influenced you very strongly. Is there someone who comes to mind?

T. My father says three words a year. He is very quiet. My mother is a non-stop talker. Maybe I got it from her. As far as learning how to communicate? Maybe I got it by being on the air. I was a regular on a TV talk show. One day that I remember well was when I was sitting in the green room with the Reverend Billy Graham. I got to sit in the green room with him, just the two of us. I said to him, "You are known by everyone, world leaders, every president. You're in this business. How do you explain your success?" He told me there are people who are better theologians than he, better ministers, people who are better at this whole business of religion than he. He said that he was given a gift of explaining the Bible *simply.* I thought about it, and I thought, "That's what I do." I explain the financial concepts simply.

{People really do like to listen to people who don't talk down to them. If you can make complex issues and ideas seem easy to others, you have stepped onto the path to success!}

W. You explain it in ways that people understand, without going over their heads?
T. When I start thinking about how I am going to explain this, I get examples and ideas in my head that say, "How about this example or this analogy?"
W. So that would be an example of a strategy that you use to make it simple. What is the strategy that you use to help them understand these concepts simply?
T. Keeping it in very simple terms. I try to use analogies a lot. I firmly believe that even though the financial dealings at General Motors are very complex, it still comes down to nothing more than the way you and I keep our checkbooks. Money in, money out. They have a lot of doors, but they are really doing the same thing you are, just at a more complicated level.
W. So that is a method, or strategy, you have of simplifying the message and breaking it down into understandable concepts. Your listener understands what you are saying. What would you say is the biggest mistake that people make in trying to communicate? You have talked to enough people to know what does not work.
T. There are people who use a lot of jargon, or try to use big words. In this business, the financial business, you don't hear those people on the air (on the radio) because they get washed out.
W. Who comes to mind?

T. I have a friend in the insurance business. He is a very bright guy. I wanted to interview him for a story I was doing on insurance. Thank goodness I had it on tape, because it was a very simple message that I wanted him to explain about insurance, and I kept having to stop him and say, "You are talking jargon. You are not communicating anything. You are talking garbage." He was never able to deliver his message without getting very complex. I know another guy in the brokerage business, and we make jokes about him to his face, about how he takes his clients hostage. Once he take clients into his office, he doesn't let go of them for hours.

W. Not a good way to have rapport!

T. He goes in and starts talking about the amortization of the scheduling of this chart and blah, blah, and the clients are there trying to figure out how to get out!

W. Why doesn't he, or someone like him, understand that this big talk goes over people's heads and makes it difficult to understand?

T. We have talked to him about this. We make jokes about his hostages when he finally lets them out. I tell him, "You are not getting anywhere with this." The hostage situation went pretty long today! Cut it out."

W. And the important thing to consider is the way it makes the clients feel. The state that they are in is the most valuable part of communication. So when you consider how important that is, the way they feel being the critical factor, what you are describing is a way to make someone feel small or inadequate or dumb.

T. Or bored! My wife and I went to a furniture store this weekend. We had a good saleswoman. She offered just the right level of help, not too pushy, but was there for us. We were looking through some books, and another salesman came over to answer a question about one of the pieces of furniture. He began to tell us about how long he had been in the furniture business. Then he launched into a story about his brother and how he got into the business, and how his brother knows this guy over here, and pretty soon we were into this guy's brother's life. And all we wanted to know about was the piece of furniture! He was off in his own world.

{We always want to communicate in the other person's world. Get on their map, if you will, and listen to what they are saying. People who constantly tell you what their experience is who aren't getting paid to do so, are going to fail in the communication process.}

W. A person like that doesn't know that his personal life is not important to you! And when he goes off into his personal stories that fascinate him, he has no clue that his listener has no desire to know about that!

T. And why can't we remember some of those rules? Why can't we remember that the favorite subject of someone is them! It is very hard in my business, in the media business. Even though it is talk radio, it is still very limited and sometimes very hard to talk about the other person. It is interactive, but still very controlled. I have to be in control and do most of the talking. So, I will interject lots of stories about a particular topic, and it becomes a lot of *me* in that. In normal social or business relationships, I like to ask people about *them.*

W. When you are in these social situations, what is your motivation to ask about them? What is your reason for wanting to get to know them personally?

T. It depends. In a business situation, if they are clients or potential clients, I want to know as much about them as possible so I can do the best I can for them.

W. And if it is someone in a social situation and you just want to create rapport, what do you do? Why do you want to know about them?

T. When I was in the army, I had a reputation as the inquisitor because everyone I met I drilled. Where did you go to school? How many brothers and sisters do you have? Where are you from? First, I want to know more about a person to decide if I want to spend more time with him or her. And secondly, I am just a very curious individual.

{Tom may or may not realize where his success originates, but notice that he comments on his being a very curious individual. This is one of the most common traits of successful people!}

W. And that might be one of the most valuable skills you have. That may be the one thing that has helped you rise to the top. When you are sincerely interested in what other people say, they know it. They feel that sincerity, and they know that you are not interested for other motives. They know that you are genuinely interested in what they have to say. Maybe you have never looked at it or analyzed it before, but if you are asking those questions because you really do want to know about them, they know you are really interested in them. And they think, "Wow, he really likes me." That may be why you have risen to the top.

T. Yes, I am genuinely interested in finding out about other people!

W. Is there a time when you were not able to do that? A time when you were at a loss for words, or that you were nervous about transitioning to another level?

T. Yes, there was. When I was a teenager. I remember as a child being in a lot of leadership roles. I was the head crossing guard, the chief altar boy, so as a child I always took these leadership roles. As a teenager I would find myself struggling to put together an articulate paragraph of conversation. I found myself getting caught up in the words "like, ya know, like, uh," and I found myself doing that and saying I have got to stop doing this! It was those crutches that I found myself using, and at that point I was consciously aware of my speech and knew that I didn't want to speak that way.

W. So that was a time when you made a conscious decision to make a change? As a teenager? That is very insightful to know you didn't want to talk like that.

T. I knew I didn't want to sound like a goofy teenager. I needed to be more articulate.

W. So, you knew you needed to make a change in order to communicate your ideas properly. Is there another time where you transitioned to another step up in your career?

T. Yes, it was with Price Waterhouse. It was my first job right out of college. All of our clients were Fortune 500 companies. I sat in boardrooms with the senior partners. The senior partner would go over our tax analysis, and I was the one who knew where the dots of the I's were. My boss would ask me from time to time to speak up about certain things that I knew. In doing so, I would sometimes say things bluntly. I was slamming these sentences out. He collared me one time and told me I had to be more judicious about the choice of the words I used. I never forgot it!

{How many times have you talked to people who said, "Well, gee, I was just being honest." You can read that statement as, "Well, I was just being hurtful." Being unkind or speaking out without anything to back your statements up is rarely the right move in the communication process.}

W. What was your reaction to his comments?

T. I thought they were great!

W. Many people would have felt defensive about that. It might have created resistance or resentment. For you, wanting to be a great communicator, you felt it was great, and now that you know, you can do something about it.

T. Well, he was right. Exactly. He cared enough about me to tell me, and he was willing to tell me bluntly that I had to be more judicious about my choice of words.

W. So how did you do that? How did you make that change?

T. It is in the words. When you have a choice of words and you are considering a harsh word, you get your mental thesaurus out and find a new word.

W. I understand that. I have been guilty of the same thing in the past, and I now have a little switch in my brain that stops and chooses a new word.

T. Yes, yes. It's amazing how quickly the brain can check that mental thesaurus and find a new word.

W. A lot of people sabotage that ability by assuming that they can't think of a word, by saying their memory is bad, or by saying they can't remember the word they need.

T. You are right. I've seen people stop and say I can't think of that word.

W. At that point you create a block or put up a wall that actually prevents you from thinking of it, almost like giving yourself a hypnotic suggestion that you will, in fact, not be able to think of that word. That it won't come to you. So, instead, you can suggest that it will come to you in a moment, and at least create the possibility that the word will come to you. Do you have another level that you aspire to? I think in terms of outcomes, rather than goals, and I wonder what outcomes you have in your future.

T. I am very bad at that. I know goal setting is important, but I am very bad at that.

W. Generally, we need an outcome that we can see very clearly, that we can move toward. For many, it is like they have car and a map, but they don't follow directions and just drive around in circles.

T. I know it is important, and I give that same speech in seminars about how you can't just go out and invest helter skelter, no more than you could just get in the car without knowing where you are going. But I live my life that way.

W. And yet you never had that plan? The plan that said I want to be in the media, or I want to make it in the financial market?

T. Nope. The way I got involved in finance is this. I grew up in the inner city. I grew up in a very low-income neighborhood. I had no role models other than people struggling, blue-collar wage earners.

W. So, what decision did you make as a result of that? The decision that pushed you ahead?

T. I didn't! I did not know we were that poor. There was a girl I was interested in as a teenager, and she lived on the other side of town. She was in an upscale neighborhood and I liked that. Then when I worked for Price Waterhouse they had very high expectations for everyone and everything in the firm. I was flying first class, staying in the nicest hotels. I went to resorts, and I liked it! I had not seen this before!

W. And right there, with your eyes wide open, you realized that there is a whole other world? Did you make a decision about your life at that point that you wanted to be part of that world?

T. Nope! No, I didn't.

W. Well, you defy all logic.

T. I just went roaring down that road and said "I like this!" It is that entrepreneurial spirit. You have to have your eyes and ears open. You have to be willing to give up what you've got. I gave up Price Waterhouse for a client who came to me and said we want to make you our chief financial officer. I thought, gee, that's great, but the new company didn't acknowledge the prestige I had with PW. I went from this real Marine Corps thing to Price Waterhouse, where everybody was very proud, and anybody who works for them is quite accomplished. But, that was not good enough.

W. So you couldn't stay where you were?

T. That wasn't good enough. I wanted to do something new and exciting.

{One type of successful person becomes bored fairly easily and enjoys the process of change. Tom clearly is one of these people, and that is an important concept to be aware of!}

W. Even though you didn't know what the next thing was, you knew you wanted the new thing. You found you couldn't stay in any one thing very long?

T. I stayed in finance but there is another life. The media is another industry. It offers me escape from one to the other. I look at opportunities, where I think most people go down the path and just do the same thing.

W. Following the path of least resistance, then?

T. I think they are not willing, or don't have the nerve to open the door when opportunity knocks. Open the door and go through it! Don't even ask, "Who's there?" Take a risk. So I left PW knowing that if I screwed up there were other firms that would take me. I had a safety net.

W. What do you do with difficult people? How do you handle people who are argumentative or defensive?

T. Repeat their words.

W. That is called pacing. It is a great strategy.

T. Someone told me that years ago and I tried it, and it worked magically. It is like putting up the mirror to that person who is talking to you when they are upset.

W. Let me ask you my favorite question. If you had the power to change anything, what would you most like to change?

T. Remember, I am someone who doesn't know what I am doing tomorrow. I am just as happy as I can be. Not a thing. I love my life.

W. And all because you know how to talk your way to the top!

T. And I don't mind making mistakes. We all have our issues and problems, and I don't mind those that work with me making mistakes. If I wanted to change anything, I suppose I would change human nature. I know there is a reason for most things. Even with President Clinton, there is a reason for his behavior. This nation is long overdue in having a conversation about morals. For the first time families are asking, "What about lying? What about cheating?" So I look at it and go . . . .

W. You could look at it as a gift, then?

T. It wasn't a good thing in itself, and I don't want to be a pollyanna, but I tend to look for the positive in it. What can we learn from this?

What can we learn from Tom Sullivan? We learn that mistakes are mistakes and not failures. We learn that when we are given feedback we want to listen to it. We learn that opportunities knock and if you are ready to change and jump at the opportunity, you can scale the ladder quite quickly. Success can seem like an accident, but successes leave clues. The people who achieve greatness talk to others in a simple and kind manner. They are curious. They are sincerely interested in what makes other people tick. They are willing to seize opportunity, and they are teachable. Tom Sullivan is a bit unusual in that he says he doesn't know what he wants tomorrow to be like. But I suspect that he will do just fine! Thanks, Tom, for letting us inside the mind of one of America's best communicators!

CHAPTER 16

Who Gets to the Top?

EVOLUTIONARY PSYCHOLOGY IS THE STUDY of how we relate to each other as humans based on principles of genetics and evolution. This chapter touches on the cutting edge of understanding human communication and just who makes it to the top.

There are a few multi-billion-dollar corporations that know how to reach the inborn genetic programming within each of us so we will be inclined to purchase their products. You are going to now learn a few of the secrets of these international successes. The world's best advertising is not geared just to our behavior, but to something that is next to impossible to change: our DNA. What you are going to learn in this chapter is how to apply the research that we have done in corporate marketing and selling to your everyday life.

All people need food, clothing, and shelter in our society. Those are inborn programs. We must eat to survive. We must have clothing to survive the cold winters. We must have some kind of shelter for inborn needs of security and territorial ownership. Beyond this, there are very few other inborn needs, but there are many inborn tendencies that drive human behavior as your customer grows and becomes an adult.

Appeal to the Benefit of the Many

Our genes do not simply generate the tendency for us to survive and care for self, but they virtually command and carry out a powerful compulsion to care for the larger groups that we are part of. In fact, just about everyone's genetic makeup is such that we are programmed to help the larger group carry on and thrive.

Have you ever seen a news story where a man raced into a burning building to save a young child? Not only is that an altruistic act, it is part of most people's genetic programming. The compulsion to care for others in our group is very powerful.

Almost all people are programmed to act in the best interests of the following:

- Themselves
- The Family
- The Group
- Society
- God

One big mistake that salespeople make is that they only appeal to the customer's best interest when they should be appealing to the customer's interest in how their product will help his family, his employees, his civic groups and his church organization, society as a whole, and even God. It was only in 1998 that scientists discovered a portion of the brain that is activated when communicating with a Divine Being.

There is a McDonald's commercial that illustrates how to appeal to the greater genetic needs. The theme song that says, "You deserve a break today, so get up and get away, to McDonalds . . ." plays in the background. The image is of a man who has had a long day at work and the theme initially plays to his deserving a break. The motivator, however, is not self satisfaction. The motivator is dad and mom and the kids all driving off to McDonald's together.

> *What a person may not be able to justify for himself can often be justified if it becomes obvious that it benefits our family, or society, or the group to which we belong.*

Competition is a Driving Force of Survival

The field of evolutionary psychology has taught us that competition between individuals and groups is what naturally selects winners and losers in society. When you are asking your customer to purchase your products and services, appeal, subtly, on the grounds that owning your products or services will give him an advantage in society, within the group, or against his competitors. The makeup of the individual is to sur-vive competitively. The world's greatest competitors are those who become the wealthiest individuals. Bill Gates, Ted Turner, Warren Buffett. All of these men are very good people, yet brilliant competitors. Bill Gates doesn't seek to own a share of the market with Microsoft. He seeks to dominate the market and does so by providing outstanding products at reasonable prices. You can do the same by appealing to the competitive nature in your customers. Do so quietly and with careful subtlety. *It is a fact that those who opt out of competition reduce their level of prestige on the societal ladder.*

Success, survival, and failure at all levels of animal and human soci-ety are wrapped up in the ability to compete and dominate.

Selling to Groups Is Far Easier Than to Individuals

It is a known fact that madness is the exception in individuals and far more common in groups. Most normal humans would never throw ice balls at unprotected, innocent people walking down the street. Watching a football game in season would never convince you of this truth, as refer-ees are constantly on the lookout for spectators, who they know can gen-erate great harm. Fans have been seen on numerous occasions to literally kill people at soccer games because of the intensity generated during the competitiveness of the game.

Every public speaker knows that persuading most of the people in a large group of people is far easier than persuading one individual in a one-on-one setting. There is often an IQ deficiency in groups. Group think takes over, and people will follow the most vocal proponents of a proposition. Most people are like sheep waiting for the shepherds.

Scientific research clearly shows that the more people there are in a group, the more likely the vast majority of the group will comply with whatever the leader is proposing. The fascinating caveat is that there is a common fear of speaking and presenting before groups. This gives the master salesperson who is adept at communicating a powerful edge over others in the selling process.

People often act like animals in groups and are easily herded. Even the master of communication cannot expect or even consider having 100 percent assent in group settings. In all groups, there are individuals who rise above group think. When facing their objections, always honor and respect their points of view and continue with your presentation. The vast majority will always rule, and you will nearly always succeed in group selling situations if you follow all the key elements and pull all the right strings.

Remember the truism from the nineteenth century: The larger the lynch mob, the more brutal the lynching. Those in an emotional frenzy lose all sense of ethics. Think of experiences that you have had that make this fact clear to you.

Those in group settings tend to be led by the unconscious minds of the rest of the group. The average intelligence of the unconscious mind is about that of a six-year-old. This doesn't mean that there isn't a vast array of information stored in the unconscious mind. Indeed there is. It does mean that the unconscious mind is far more reactive and emotional than the analytical, conscious mind. The conscious mind rests in group settings, making an easy target for the ethical salesperson or the unethical swindler.

It is encoded in people's genetic makeup to seek safety in groups. Once in a group, the normal person's defenses are dropped, as there is a feeling of safety in almost all of the group.

Appealing to the Quest for Affiliation

All humans need to feel wanted. Science and medical research clearly reveals that feeling unwanted stunts all forms of human growth and development. Physical, psychological, and emotional growth all are influenced by a person's perception of feeling wanted. In fact, people who say they don't need to feel wanted are literally lying or psychotic. The need is preprogrammed.

You need to make it clear to your customers that you are interested in them as more than a customer. People can sense true interest and when they do, they are likely to develop the long-term relationships with you that will create win-win selling situations.

One recent medical study concluded that "a lack of warmth and meaningful relationships" is a significant cause of heart attacks in many people.

What does this tell us about needs that are genetically programmed into our behavior? We are physically influenced by love, compassion, and relationships.

> *It is imperative that your customer perceive you as someone who truly cares about him. He must feel a sense of compassion and interest in him before you can predictably make sales at will.*

Dr. Dean Ornish published a wealth of material in 1998 about the fact that closeness can literally heal people and separation from loved ones can kill. Understanding this biological fact helps us influence others in a powerful way, doesn't it?

Is Your Customer Happy in His Work?

Did you discover that your client doesn't like her current job? Does she think that her work is important? (This would likely have come up during the values elicitation in the selling process.)

> *If people do not believe their work is important, use this fact as leverage for them to buy your product or service, saving them from physical illness.*

Did you know that if a person doesn't think what they are doing is important, they are likely to become ill and experience numerous and lengthy illnesses? With the knowledge that this has been programmed into our thinking, the persuader holds powerful control in any process.

He Seems So Confident

There are no self confident and supremely confident people. In fact, research shows that although we may feel secure, we do not feel extremely self confident. Whenever you see a speaker who appears to be in complete control, you can know that he or she fears the same things you do. Confidence is something that can be boosted, but you will really find no supremely confident people. Therefore, when you are creating your messages or presentations, feel free to appeal to people's desire to be more confident.

Positive Attitude?

Projecting a positive attitude is not nearly as helpful to the self when contrasted with the great degree that it encourages others. When your customer sees your positive attitude, it gives him optimism and encouragement that you are a good person to be with and buy from. Generating a "positive attitude" is very important to sales success, because it improves the relationship you have with others.

Your Customer Likes Some People . . . But Not as Many as You Might Think

Your customer doesn't like many others in his group. He tolerates them. If your customer is a franchise owner, he probably has a few friends in the same franchise, but not many. Remember this as you are pacing your customer. Just because he owns a McDonald's doesn't mean he likes all the other franchise owners. He probably will be hard pressed to admit this, but just knowing this genetic pre-disposition on your part is enough to save sales for you. Within the group there are various cliques of people. The fact that everyone is in the same high school doesn't mean they will like each other. It means they will all be happy to be rivals against another school, but it doesn't in any way imply there will be friendliness within the school.

People tend to form cliques within their own larger groups. They tend to like the people in their clique. The are less interested in other people in the larger whole, and they are likely to strongly dislike those in competing groups.

What is even more interesting is how much your customer doesn't like those outside his group. If you are selling insurance to the First Church of God, you will not build rapport by noting how well the First Church of Christ liked you. In fact, you are likely to lose the sale. They are not in the same group. The more intricately they play a role within their own group, the less likely they are to like or even tolerate those in another competing group.

How the Enemy Makes a Sale for You

When it seems that there is no competitive edge to your product or service, you can utilize a genetic predisposition that was alluded to in the point discussed above. You can assist in creating an enemy to bind people together. The Internal Revenue Service is an enemy that has been able to bind the thoughts of the public together. This has been done by our elected officials so we will vote for them. The enemy can be "good" or "evil." Appearances of good and evil are in the eyes of the beholder, of course. McDonald's doesn't like Burger King. Microsoft doesn't like Netscape.

> *Create or identify an enemy that needs to be fought, and then define how you, or your product or service, will help in the fight against the common enemy. An enemy can be a person, a group, a nation, or a non-living thing, like drugs, cigarettes, associations, churches, and newspapers.*

How do you utilize this principle of genetics in your favor? President Clinton, in the wake of the Paula Jones/Monica Lewinsky hearings, was able to take the focus off himself by targeting a common enemy of almost all Americans, Saddam Hussein. The strategy of "talking war" was brilliant, uniting the nation as it had seven years earlier under the Bush Administration. The real threat of biological weapons in the hands of Iraq was enough to take Clinton/Lewinsky off the front page of the newspaper and put Hussein, United Nations inspectors, and talk of war in its place. This created a new perspective in the public's thinking about the significance of the Jones/Lewinsky scandals.

Creating or identifying a common enemy is an excellent tool for building rapport and increasing compliance. If you can help your customer become frustrated with the status quo, his likely future, or the success of his competitors, he is more likely to act in a positive manner on your request for his compliance.

The concept of using anger, disgust, fear, hatred, and negative emotions in effective selling and marketing is as old as monetary exchange.

For years we have seen commercials about how disgusting roaches are in the house. We spend billions of dollars in America on security systems every year, but most people will spend for such a system only if they have had their security violated or fear it will be. People will purchase products to relieve pain, reduce anxiety, be less depressed . . . and these products go far beyond medications! People buy magazines, books, CDs, computer games, internet services, cars, houses, and groceries, all to reduce negative emotions.

The Haves and the Have Nots

"Money doesn't bring you happiness."
"People care too much about money."
"Money isn't important."
"I don't need things."
"I don't like being around all those control freaks."
"All I need to be happy is . . ."

When you are selling, you pace the client's actions and beliefs. But remember that he is only human, and therefore is programmed like most other humans. Your customer will often state something that he really doesn't believe because he wishes that what he was saying was true.

What are the facts about control, having, and happiness? How do these biological truths relate to your selling your products and services?

> *Control: The more you have, the healthier you are. Control is what keeps you focused and aware. People who experience a great deal of control in their lives tend to be healthier. When people feel in control, or feel your product or service will put them in control, they are likely to buy from you now.*

If your customer is to succeed in life and move up the ladder of success and survival, he needs problems, the ability to solve them, and the victories that come from defeating his problems. Control is analogous to personal power. Personal power is the ability to take action and achieve. The ability to meet life's challenges head on and win is not only useful in raising self esteem and self efficacy but also improving the general health of your client!

If your product or service will give your customer more control in his life and he realizes it, then he will buy your product, period. Without control, people become hopeless. When people become hopeless you are once again able to help your customer. If your product or service can generate hope, you give new life to your customer, literally. If your customer sincerely believes that your product or service can help him, then you can help him change his life.

> *We need a significant amount of control for happiness. If you can paint a clear picture of how you can help another person regain control in some area of his life or business, he will buy anything from you.*

Who Your Customer Wants to Be Like

In all species, including humankind, the masses are compelled to be like the leader of the group(s). Your appeal to your customer therefore should in part be one of installing the desire to be like the leaders in his or her field. This could mean being a better parent, a better employee, a better supervisor. Your job is to show how your products and services help your customer be more like the leader(s) of the group(s) he is most intimately linked to. In general, we imitate our leader's behavior. As a sales person, we therefore want to show how using our products will make the customer more like the leaders.

A Key Male Consideration

Men who are rich in testosterone often find themselves either in great trouble or achieving great success. Testosterone inspires confidence and aggression. Most entrepreneurial types tend to be high in testosterone and confident of their ability to achieve in business and life. Knowing this allows you to touch on this area of human development. Appealing to the core urges of a man in some manner is useful in awakening his confidence and "go-for-it" attitudes.

> *Help your client reexperience past victories in any aspect of life and you will probably succeed in creating a "testosterone rush." Linking your product to this rush will enhance the probability of compliance.*

Testosterone is tied to "winning" in men. An excellent way to create a testosterone rush in men is to have them recount a story of a time when they overcame the odds and "won." This normally creates a testosterone surge in men and builds confidence. By successfully linking this internal state to your product or service, you almost assure yourself of making a sale.

See You at the Top

One of my all-time favorite self-development books is *See You at the Top* by Zig Ziglar. When Zig wrote the book he had little if any idea that it would go on to sell more than 1.7 million copies. Zig could have predicted such an outcome had he known the genetic propensity of people to gravitate toward leaders in a group. Not only do we want to be like the leader in a group, we also want to be *liked* by the leader in a group.

The higher up the ladder a person climbs, the more "friends" a person has. Now, it should be noted that these friends may be "fair-weather friends," but clearly those who wish to consider themselves friends of the leaders in groups are far greater than those who dwell near the bottom of the societal ladders.

Therefore you have an opportunity to appeal to an individual's programmed desire, first to be at the top of the ladder and second to be friends of the person at the top of the (or "a") ladder.

You may have the opportunity to share with your customer the idea that if he moves up the ladder in his group, his health will improve. Recent research shows that those who are higher up the "ladder" have less hypertension. Health benefits are going to be a good justification for any action in the twenty-first century. This is one that is truly worth noting when it ties in with your products and services.

People want to either be at the top, be seen with the people on top, or be given hope that they may be able to make it to the top. Your product or service should somehow be able to help your client up the ladder.

Genuinely "Nice"

There are a great number of truly nice people in this world. We have all met a true altruist. This person is willing to give you the shirt off his back, and he would literally feel blessed to do so. However, you may be surprised to know that gestures of compassion are not always the result of altruism. In fact, such is not the case in the majority of cases.

Compassionate gestures help us feel superior, often causing people to look down on benefactors. In fact, not only are those who give doing so for a heightened sense of importance, but those on the receiving end rarely gain the long-term appreciation of those who helped them. Resentment, oddly, is often the result.

An example of this occurs on a macro level. Over the last several decades, America has given or loaned numerous countries billions upon billions of dollars. What is the normal attitude of the countries that have been the beneficiaries of these loans and donations? Many of them hate America passionately.

When appropriate, you may find it useful to appeal to the feelings of strength a person gets from doing "a good thing," in addition to the feeling of "goodness" a person experiences when helping others.

The Best of Times . . . the Worst of Times

When times are relatively good, on average, we are biologically programmed to venture out and increase risk and adventure in our lives. When times are bad, on average, we are likely to play our cards closer to the vest and be much more conservative.

When participating in the sales process, it is very useful to know whether your client is going through good times or bad times. If he is experiencing good times, you can appeal to his desire to experiment, his need to expand his horizons and explore. If he is trying to cope with bad times, you need show how your products will allow him to meet his conservative needs.

The emotional appeal of your product is important in determining whether you will make the sale or not. People will justify their purchase logically, but first they need to fit the product into their emotional filters.

Appeal to your customer's need to take risks and participate in adventure in good times. When experiencing bad times, appeal to your client's needs of security and safety.

The fields of evolutionary psychology and behavioral genetics are just beginning to be understood. There is much to learn about who makes it to the top and what communication skills will be necessary. In this chapter we have touched on the beginning. To keep abreast of current trends, you may contact the author at the address listed on the last page of this book.

CHAPTER 17

Sell Your Way to the Top in the 21st Century

HAVING WORKED IN SALES in one capacity or another for twenty-five years, I feel it necessary to give some current insights into communicating specifically in the sales process for all the sales people who will read this book! Sales people really make the world go around. Their job is one of the toughest in the world. There is a reward for the challenges of selling. Sales has more millionaires per capita than any other field! This is an area where hard work and smart work really pay off. Here then are the keys to sales success in the twenty-first century!

1. Managing Your State of Mind in All Situations

Your state of mind is one element of the sales process over which you have a great deal of control. Your "state" is generally considered to be made up of three elements, two of which you can control and one of which is difficult to control.

A. YOUR INTERNAL REPRESENTATIONS

There is no question that the pictures, words, and emotions you experience in your mind are in large part under your control. If your internal representations are sabotaging you, then you need to take back control of your mind. You must begin to paint new pictures for yourself. Begin to see your life as more likely to succeed. Begin to see yourself as becoming competent in understanding the behavior, actions, and thinking of other people. Realize that as you become effective in understanding the workings of others, you become more in control of yourself.

Your internal representations include what you say to yourself when you talk. These representations include the tone of voice you use when you talk to yourself. *If you don't like what is going on in your brain, change it now.* You can change the tone of your voice when you talk to you from one that implies "You Dummy" to one that commands, "You ARE going to make it BIG!"

When you experience pictures that create a sense of hopelessness, immediately change the picture to a struggle that ends with your success instead of failure. Taking an active role in your self management is very important to your success as a highly effective salesperson.

B. PHYSIOLOGY

Managing your mind is inextricably linked to managing your body. If you are obese, suffer from aches and pains that can be attended to, and notice that your day-to-day posture and "carrying of yourself" is poor, you must take action to change now.

Overweight? Start a weight reduction program immediately. Your body image directly affects your self esteem, and that means it affects your sales. *Become active and get your body image in line so you are proud of the way you look. How you see yourself impacts your attractiveness to others.*

Do you suffer from pains, aches, and other somatics that can be treated or helped with therapy? Do it! Pain and other somatics reduce your effectiveness and drain you of necessary energy that you need to give to your customers.

Is your posture lousy? Start sitting up straight and walking as if someone has a huge hand pushing your buttocks forward. This will improve your posture dramatically. The way you carry yourself will change many "nos" into "yeses" because many people perceive that a hunched-over appearance is indicative of low self confidence. When people think you are not confident, it drains their confidence in you as a salesperson and reduces your sales volume.

C. GENETIC FACTORS CAN BE HELPED, TOO!

If you suffer from depression, anxiety, panic disorder, and other emotional challenges, talk to your medical doctor and find appropriate medications. There is no shame in utilizing anti-depressants and anti-anxiety medications to make up for inefficient neurobiology. It is very difficult to change your "brain chemistry" in a predictable manner with cognitive techniques alone. Take advantage of the laser beam-like medications that are available to help you. Consult your physician. There is ALWAYS something you can do.

2. Managing Your Customer's State of Mind

You can begin to manage other people's minds once you have your own state managed. Managing your customer's states is accomplished in the same manner that you manage your own state of mind.

A. INTERNAL REPRESENTATIONS

If your client needs to experience a brief dose of status quo misery to help him change to a brighter future, then you are obligated to paint a vivid picture of both what he must move away from and what he must move toward. Make the voices he is going to hear in his mind clear and loud. Help him feel the pain of stasis and the pleasure of change if he can't do it for himself.

B. PHYSIOLOGY

Sometimes it is necessary to get your client to move to create internal change in his state of mind. Hand him something. Give him a book and have him turn the pages. Ask your client to participate in some activity with you. DO SOMETHING with your client. You are not obligated to always sit face to face, across the table from each other.

If your client is in a "stuck state," the sale is going to be lost if you don't change that condition. Sometimes it is appropriate to get up and leave, or at least move somewhere else. Changing your client's physiology will change his internal state.

C. APPEAL TO YOUR CLIENT'S GENETIC MAKEUP

3. Gather, Manage and Implement Intelligence

Eliciting values, beliefs, and feelings is a method of gathering vital intelligence about your customer. The best salespeople gather intelligence about their customers before they meet, if possible. In this book you have learned about personality and buying types and who buys based upon what metaprograms. That is intelligence. There is more to be learned, however.

If you are selling to corporations, you can uncover everything from corporate earnings to corporate strategy by simply making phone calls to the company and asking before you go on your visit. Learn what you can about the needs, interests, and wants of the company.

Secretaries are a fountain of knowledge. One of my favorite selling strategies is to not bypass the secretary but instead make friends with her.

"Hi, Jane, this is Kevin Hogan, the author of *Talk Your Way to the Top*. Does your boss decide what speakers to bring into your corporation, or is there someone else I should talk to?"

"Once I get him on the phone, what does he look for in a good speaker?"

"Does he really go for motivational speakers or those who present more practical applications in sales and marketing?"

"Who was your favorite speaker in the last year or two?"

"Who was his favorite speaker in the last couple years?"

This gathering of intelligence can be powerful. In this example, you are speaking with the secretary, who is indeed the gatekeeper in the corporate world. Instead of passing by the gatekeeper, you have made friends by asking for her opinions and building a sense of respect for her and her knowledge about her company. This is how you want to gather intelligence beyond the more general buying profiles we discussed earlier in the book.

4. Networking Your Way to Sales Success

Networking works only if you have at least one of three things: You are the best in your business, you have great products, and/or you have great services. If you can meet someone's needs time and again, then you can network your way to sales success.

One excellent rule is to do something to help someone else's career every day. If you can help others with their families, businesses, or careers, you will eventually reap the rewards of what you have sowed. Networking is more than keeping a fat Rolodex. Networking is the ability to recommend someone who can solve someone else's problem. People appreciate you when you help them and have nothing to gain in return.

Assist people every day with random or intentional acts of kindness, and you will build a network of friends and people who will help you in your future. It is almost impossible to help people every day and not experience the rewards of networking down the line.

Networking also demands that you have the courage to call the people who can make a difference in your career. Many people will not call on the right person to buy or even for advice simply because they believe the celebrity won't talk to an humble salesperson. This is nonsense. At least 10 to 20 percent of celebrities, CEOs, and political leaders are reachable. If what you have to offer is useful enough, you can get your minutes with the biggest decision makers.

Be willing to be bold and occasionally embarrassed in exchange for the benefits of being known by the "right people."

5. Be a Hunter

The world's greatest salespeople don't simply sit back and wait for business to come to them. The world's greatest become adept at hunting for those who will buy their products and services. Business is *always* good for someone. Business can almost always be good *for you.*

One distinction between those who have great success in sales and those who are work-a-day salespeople is the hunter mentality. The hunter is always looking for people he can help. The hunter is relentless in the pursuit of the right groups and markets for his products and services. The hunter doesn't rely on lead sources from inside the company. The hunter is constantly developing his own contacts.

People who succeed in multi-level marketing are those who see opportunity for almost everyone they meet. This doesn't mean the hunter is pushy or involves people in a project that won't be in the individual's best interest. It does mean that a hunter will always be aware of people's needs and desires.

The hunter always goes the extra mile. When you go the extra mile, you always have more opportunities for success than the average salesperson. Going the extra mile can mean asking for referrals, or better, asking who else will definitely benefit from an outstanding product or service. The hunter is always bending over backward to help others. The hunter is generally thought of as "lucky" because he seems to regularly be meeting opportunity with preparation, one definition of luck.

6. Building Credibility with Your Customers

When communicating with your clients, is it apparent that you have their best interests in mind? If you have any doubt that you are selling a great product or service, you must choose a product or service that is great to sell. If you are selling yourself as a consultant, then you must be the best. You must constantly go the extra mile to make yourself part of the top 20 percent. This is where credibility begins.

An excellent way to establish credibility is to point out a shortcoming of your product or service and make certain that your customer sees that one flaw. Once you have done this, you have not only established credibility but you have already dealt with what is normally the only objection to your making the sale, except money issues, which may or may not be easily solved.

Remember the call letters: WII-FM. They stand for "What's in it for me?" If you can put yourself in your customer's shoes and answer that question with a laundry list of benefits, you will begin making more sales, higher volume sales, and a higher percentage of sales.

How do you appear less than credible on occasion?

Sometimes in the sales process we get nervous, fearing that our product may not be the best for our client, but we continue to sell anyway. It is at this point that you must ask your customer, "If this product could only help you to this certain degree at this price, is it something that would be really useful to you?"

If he says "yes," you can allow the pangs of nervousness to leave. If he says "no," then forget making the sale. You could still choose to pull all the right psycho-emotional strings, walk away with a check, but you will have created a Win-Lose, and that means your career will take a step backward. *Never, ever enter into any sales transaction where one party loses.*

Creating beliefs (i.e. levels of certainty) is critical. If you expect to fail, you probably will. If you expect to succeed you probably will. What you say to yourself in private is what you become. Begin to see yourself as a provider, a helper, a caretaker, a creator of value. If this isn't possible, you are selling the wrong product.

You will have a difficult time selling a particular make of cars if you don't believe that they are the best cars for the money in the business. Believe it or move to a different dealership. Refuse to sell what is second best. Never compromise your integrity. People will talk about you and believe in you if you are the best, selling products that have great value. Once you are selling something you believe in, your enthusiasm will be contagious.

Your potential in selling, and that of all of your competitors, is related to beliefs. These beliefs fall into two distinct categories. First, ethical selling demands that you believe in your idea, product, or service. Second, it must be evident that you KNOW that you are creating value by partaking in the sales process. If you feel tainted by selling, then consider how your customers will feel if they are buying someone else's products and services. Are your customers going to be buying second best if someone else goes to see them? Don't let it happen.

Being believable is about being congruent. Remember when Kathleen Willey appeared on "60 Minutes" in 1998 and clearly but emotionally told of her encounter with President Clinton at the White House? America believed her because she was congruent. She was perceived as congruent because what she said matched how she said it. Her verbal communication matched her non-verbal communication. She was believable.

Once you reach the point that you are congruent with what you are persuading another to do, you will be unstoppable.

Exercise:
Name some congruent people. Describe specifically why you believe these people to be congruent.

Name some incongruent people. Describe specifically why you believe these people to be incongruent.

What can you do so you stay in the category of congruent people?

If you are not perceived as congruent and believable, you will not make the sale. If you are perceived as believable and you sell excellent products and services, you will be on the road to success in selling. Your enthusiasm about the home you are selling, the stocks you are touting, the automobiles your customers are going to drive away in is going to be transferred to your customer like a mind virus (a meme).

Your level of certainty, combined with pure rapport and meeting true wants and needs, allows you to sell at will.

7. Develop a Sense of Fascination

Decide that you will learn everything about your customer that he is willing to comfortably share with you. Develop a sense of fascination about the work and livelihood of others. What is grand about your customers? What is great about their jobs? What is fascinating about their philosophy of life? Allow yourself to become curious and excited about learning about other people and their interests. Remember that what is interesting to you is likely to be boring to most other people. What is interesting to your customer, on the other hand, is something he can talk about for hours on end. Your customer's interests become your new areas of fascination and curiosity.

8. Change the Buying Frame

Everyone looks at "things" from his or her own point of view, from their own perspective. Key Number 8 will help you learn how to alter the way someone is looking at something so you can alter how they feel about that self same "thing." Framing is analogous to how you are going to communicate. What may seem to be a disaster for a client can be reframed as an opportunity for change and growth. What may be seen as the end of a long, sad marriage could be reframed into the beginning of a new happy life.

REFRAMING

Reframing is taking lemons and making lemonade. Reframing allows you to help someone see something they perceive as a problem that really may be an opportunity in disguise. Read the examples below, then write out common objections to your products and services and "reframe" them so you never have to think about doing this "on the spot."

Example: If you are working with "big picture people," you will now see the value of reframing (creating an area of focus) "things" in a manner where they are small and barely worth consideration or where they are large and life changing.

"You know, John, I realize that $197 per year for life insurance doesn't seem to be much to think about, but it really is important that you do this now because of the unpredictability of life and death."

or

"You know, John, I realize that $18 per month can be seen as quite a bit of money. But that is why you MUST decide to do this. If anything happens to you, your wife will have a check for $100,000 waiting for her to take care of your kids. What greater gift can you give?"

Obviously, frames help us see an issue from a different point of view than the one we just saw. Frames are used in hypnotherapy and neurolmagnetic programs to enhance and control the communication process. (Erickson, Rossi, Bandler, Grinder, Robbins, et al.) Here are a few different kinds of frames and how to utilize them in putting your products and services—and yourself—in the best light possible with your clients.

THE "AS IF" FRAME

Have you ever had a client who said, "I don't know what will happen if . . ."? It may be that you have heard something like, "I don't know what my wife would say if I . . ."

When you face these unknowns, the most effective strategy is to utilize the "As If" Frame. You can utilize this by asking one or more of these three pattern questions:

If you did this X, what would happen?

Imagine that we were successful at X. Then what would happen?

If you did decide to do "this" (agree to "this"), what was it that would have changed your mind?

These patterns are so powerful that normally the customer's objection or worry will be drained right from his mind as he answers the question.

PREFRAMING

You will recall that pointing out a minor flaw in your product or company can be a very useful tool in the sales process. It gives you immense credibility. Always, always, handle the problem that is likely to come up, in advance of the problem (objection/perceived, argument, obvious other point of view). Deal with any challenge early in the sales meeting while the significance of any issue will be considered to be very small and seemingly irrelevant.

Persuasion and influence are in large part an issue of controlling the frame of communication. You must realize that unless a person dismisses you out of hand, they see something they like about what you offer. Therefore, control that frame, that focus of attention, and key in on this area. In any disagreement, argument, or objection, you must change the focus of attention of the other person or people.

Example:

"The Psychology of Persuasion Weekend may not be the ideal weekend sales and persuasion course for you. It is possible that you will consider the price tag of $1,000 too great an investment in return for control of your life and a dramatic near-term increase in income. The weekend is about people who want to be happy, in charge of their lives and their communication. The weekend workshop is for people who want to be influential because they offer something unique to the world. If this isn't you, then simply don't come."

DEFRAMING

Jim Pickens, the author of the most powerful sales book in history, *Closers,* calls deframing the "take-away close." Once you are skilled in advanced communication techniques, you will have the confidence and ability to prudently utilize deframing.

Deframing is a linguistic tool that can only be effectively implemented when you know a person's match/mismatch meta program, or when you know the person definitely wants your service, product, or offer. In a nutshell, you give the customer one opportunity to purchase your product or hire you. If they don't, you make it explicitly clear that you will move on and allow others to take advantage of your services.

This is the basic deframing pattern:

"It makes no difference to me whether you buy this X or not. You have until tomorrow to make a decision and reserve your X. If I don't hear from you by noon, I'll know you didn't want it. No pressure. Bye."

9. Uncover Conditions to Confirmation

Even the greatest product in the world may not be able to help a person with a condition. You may be able to sell a $300,000 home at half price, which is a bargain no one is likely to ever experience. But if your client doesn't have the money for the down payment and hasn't got the income, resources, or ability to make the loan for other reasons, you have a condition. And you should never ask a person to enter into an agreement where he will lose. Value is important, but it is not the only element in deciding whether to make a sale. If the client cannot do something, don't ask him to. A condition exists in some selling situations. And when a condition does exist, you won't let that sale happen. It's a Win-Lose.

If you sense your customer has a condition, simply ask, "Is there something I'm missing that I should know about that is causing you to wonder about this product?" If he responds with some concern, address the concern and let him own your product. If he responds with a condition, don't let him buy your product. There will be another day for both of you.

10. Develop Logical Reasoning for Buying Your Product after an Emotional Decision to Do So Has Taken Place

People will buy your products and services based upon their desires in most cases. You need to develop a step-by-step process that will assist your client to bridge the gap between emotion and logical reasoning to purchase your product. You should have several series of thought processes that you have prepared for your client to consider.

If you are selling a home and your client has met the requirements to buy the home, you have a potential sale. If your client falls in love with the home, you have an emotional sale. Your job is now to move your client from emotional thought to logical justification for purchasing this home.

How can you go from logical to emotional?

First, you can ask if this is a home the client would really love to live in. An affirmative response leads you to your next question, which is: "Are you aware that every dollar you spend on your monthly house payment works for you in one way or another? Either it goes toward the principle, which means *the money comes back to you,* or you can use the rest of the payment as a tax deduction, which means *some of the money comes back to you.* When you pay rent, all of the money goes away from you, down the toilet, flushed into the sanitation system forever. The question is, do you want to own a home, or do you want to make someone else wealthy instead of developing your own wealth?"

You move from an emotional response to a logical rationale to an integration of emotions and logic. This is ethical, it is honest, and it is in the best interest of your client if no conditions exist.

11. Know When to "Close" and When to Leave

Most salespeople believe that you "close" the sale after the sales presentation is over. That is not correct. You close the sale the moment the customer wants to buy, and not a second later. When the customer is ready, you let him agree to buy your product. You have him sign the papers and take ownership. Shortly thereafter, you leave. If the customer asks you for a lunch date, that is one thing. If he is busy and has a schedule to keep, make the sale happen and then politely but with efficiency wrap up your business. In many cases, I have made the sale, had the client write a check, put it away in my briefcase, and then had lunch with the client. In situations such as this, you do not discuss your business. You continue to develop the long-term friendship by focusing on the client and his loves and interests.

In general, when your client is non-verbally or verbally telling you he wants to hire you or wants your product, let him buy it now. Then, after you have taken care of business, take care of any post-closing activities and thank your new customer.

Finally, remember, whether in the sales setting or with your lover, all of your communications must result in Win/Win or it's no deal. Anything less is simply not acceptable!

I wish you great success in applying all of these secrets to talking your way to the top!

Bibliography

Aronson, Eliot. *The Social Animal.* New York, N.Y.: W. H. Freeman and Co., 1995.

Bloom, Howard. *The Lucifer Principle: A Scientific Expedition into the Forces of History.* N.Y.: Atlantic Monthly Press, 1995.

Burgoon, Judee, Buller, David, and Woodall, W. Gill. *Nonverbal Communication: The Unspoken Dialogue.* New York, N.Y.: McGraw Hill, 1996.

Burgoon, Judee, Stern, Lisa, and Dillman, Leesa. *Interpersonal Adaptation: Dyadic Interaction Patterns.* Cambridge, England: University of Cambridge Press.

Carnegie, Dale. *How to Win Friends and Influence People.* 1936. Reprint. New York: Pocket Books, 1990.

Dalai Lama. *The Art of Happiness: A Handbook for Living.* New York, N.Y.: Riverhead Books, 1998.

Frankl, Viktor. *Man's Search for Meaning.* New York, N.Y.: Washington Square Press, 1984.

Friedman, Norman. *Bridging Science and Spirit.* St. Louis, Mo.: Living Lakes Books, 1990.

Hill, Napoleon. *Think and Grow Rich.* New York, N.Y.: Ballantine Books, 1960.

Hill, Napoleon. *The Laws of Success.* Evanston, Ill.: Success Unlimited, 1977.

Hogan, Kevin L. *The Gift: A Discovery of Happiness, Fulfillment, and Love.* Eagan, Minn.: Network 3000 Publishing Co., 1998.

Hogan, Kevin L. *The Psychology of Persuasion: How to Persuade Others to Your Way of Thinking.* Gretna, La.: Pelican Publishing Co., 1996.

Hogan, Kevin L. *Life By Design: Your Handbook for Transformational Living.* Eagan, Minn.: Network 3000 Publishing, 1995.

Holy Bible. King James Version.

Horton, William. *Primary Objective.* Eschaton Books, 1998.

Jung, Carl. *Psychological Types.* New York: Harcourt, Brace, 1923.

Keyes, Ken. *Handbook to Higher Consciousness.* Coos Bay, Ore., 1991.

Kiersey, David. *Please Understand Me.* Del Mar, Calif.: Prometheus Nemesis Book Co., 1978.

Knapp, Mark, and Hall, Judy. *Nonverbal Communication in Human Interaction.* 3rd ed. Fort Worth: Harcourt, Brace College Publications, 1992.

Leathers, Dale. *Successful Nonverbal Communication.* Needham Hts., Mass.: Allyn and Bacon, 1997.

Myers, Isabel Briggs. *Introduction to Type: A Description of the Theory and Application of the Myers-Briggs Type Indicator.* Palo Alto, Calif.: Consulting Psychologists Press, 1987.

Palmer, Harry. *ReSurfacing.* Altamonte Springs, Fla.: Star's Edge, 1994.

Robbins, Anthony. *Unlimited Power.* New York, N.Y.: Ballantine Books, 1986.

Seligman, Martin. *Learned Optimism.* New York, N.Y.: Alfred Knopf, 1991.

Simonton, Dean. *Greatness.* New York, N.Y.: Guilford Press, 1994.

Sumner, Holly. *The Meditation Sourcebook.* New York, N.Y., 1999.

Thurston, Mark. *Edgar Cayce Handbook for Creating Your Future.* New York, N.Y.: Ballantine Books, 1992.

Wilber, Ken. *Sex, Ecology, Spirituality, The Spirit of Evolution.* Boston, Mass.: Shambala, 1995.

Wolinsky, Stephen. *Quantum Consciousness: The Guide to Experiencing Quantum Psychology.* Norfolk, Conn.: Bramble Books, 1993.

Wright, Robert. *The Moral Animal: Why We Are the Way We Are: The New Science of Evolutionary Psychology.* N.Y.:Vintage, 1994.

Ziglar, Zig. *See You at the Top.* Gretna, La.: Pelican Publishing Co., 1984.

Contact the Author

COMMUNICATION IS THE KEY TO SUCCESS in business, passionate interpersonal relationships, and even one's own internal happiness. Would you like to get on the Success Dynamics mailing list to be kept abreast of cutting-edge communication advances? Do you want to bring Kevin Hogan to your company or group as a speaker or trainer? You may call or write him at:

Kevin Hogan, Psy.D.
3432 Denmark #108
Eagan, MN 55123
(612) 616-0732
Web site: http//www.kevinhogan.com
E-mail: khogan1652@aol.com